CULTURES OF THE WORLD®

ARMENIA

Sakina Dhilawala

Marshall Cavendish
Benchmark

New York

PICTURE CREDITS

Cover photo: © Dean Conger / CORBIS

age fotostock / R. MATINA: 51 • age fotostock / WOJTEK BUSS: 17, 21, 53, 55, 58, 68, 104, 111, 124 • alt.TYPE / Reuters: 32, 35, 41, 64, 107 • ArmenPress: 18, 34, 37, 65, 99, 102 (top), 103 • Audrius Tomonis: 135 • Bes Stock: 5, 43, 44, 96, 106 • Bill Wassman / Lonely Planet Images: 3, 4, 20, 38, 78, 118, 129 • Björn Klingwall: 79, 92, 122 • Camera Press: 63, 100 • Eye Ubiquitous / Hutchison: 56, 110 • Hulton Getty Picture Collection: 24, 28, 29 (top), 77, 84 • Hutchison Library: 7, 10, 13, 14, 19, 29 (bottom), 30, 31, 42, 45, 47, 50, 61, 62, 69, 73, 74, 80, 83, 97, 101, 112, 115, 119, 121, 123, 127 • Image Bank: 15, 16 • John Walmsley: 11, 12, 40, 72, 91, 105 • Levon Parian: 71, 109, 113 • Life File: 48 • MARKA / STEFANO LUNARDI: 6, 76 • Neil Beer: 33, 49, 75, 128 • North Wind: 25 • Patker Photo Agency: 66 • Photolibrary: 1, 23, 54, 57, 59, 60, 120 • Society for Cooperation in Russian & Soviet Studies: 89, 102 (bottom) • Sonia Halliday: 82, 98 • Stephane Victor / Lonely Planet Images: 52, 85, 88, 125 • STOCKFOOD / BRAUN, STEFAN: 126 • STOCKFOOD / BUNTROCK, GERRIT: 130 • STOCKFOOD / KIRCHHERR, JO: 131

PRECEDING PAGE

Armenian women displaying their fresh harvest for the day.

Publisher (U.S.): Michelle Bisson
Editors: Deborah Grahame, Mabelle Yeo, Rizza Manaois
Copyreader: Sherry Chiger
Designer: Jailani Basari
Cover picture researcher: Connie Gardner
Picture researcher: Thomas Khoo

Marshall Cavendish Benchmark
99 White Plains Road
Tarrytown, NY 10591
Web site: www.marshallcavendish.us

Originated and designed by Times Editions Private Limited
An imprint of Marshall Cavendish International (Asia) Private Limited
A member of Times Publishing Limited

All Internet sites were correct and accurate at the time of printing. All monetary figures in this publication are in U.S. dollars.

Library of Congress Cataloging-in-Publication Data
Dhilawala, Sakina, 1964–
 Armenia / Sakina Dhilawala. — 2nd ed.
  p. cm.
 Summary: "Provides comprehensive information on the geography, history, wildlife, governmental structure, economy, cultural diversity, peoples, religion, and culture of Armenia"—Provided by publisher.
 Includes bibliographical references and index.
  ISBN 978-0-7614-2029-3
 1. Armenia (Republic)—Juvenile literature. 2. Armenia (Republic)—History—Juvenile literature.
 3. Armenia (Republic)—Civilization—Juvenile literature. I. Title.
DK685.6.D48 2007
947.56—dc22   2007014890

Printed in China

9 8 7 6 5 4 3 2 1

CONTENTS

The Sardarapat Battle Memorial that was constructed in Yerevan in 1968.

The intricate entrance to a church in the town of Echmiadzin. Considered to be the most holy place in Armenia, Echmiadzin is home to the Supreme Patriarch of the Armenian Apostolic Church.

INTRODUCTION

ARMENIA WAS THE FIRST country in the world to formally adopt Christianity. A powerful people, Armenians in ancient times had the tenacity to challenge the Roman, Byzantine, Arab, Persian, and Ottoman empires. Armenian history is in fact marked by struggles for independence and domination by foreign powers. Armenia today is home to nearly 3 million people, about 96 percent of whom are ethnic Armenians. Minority communities include Russians, Kurds, and Jews. Today Armenians are considered the most dynamic of the peoples of the former Soviet Union. Their country has an outstanding economic growth rate, and its standards in education and medical science are on par with those of Western European countries.

Armenians are sociable, hospitable, and faithful to family and community ties. Most Armenians have a pronounced religious belief and are deeply attached to their national church, the Armenian Apostolic Church. Armenians are also first-rate farmers and outstanding craftspeople, excelling in handicraft, sculpture, and fine work in precious metals and textiles.

GEOGRAPHY

ALMOST TWO-THIRDS of Armenia, with its mighty mountains topped with snow, one great lake, and countless ravines and canyons, can be classified as unfit for settled habitation. Large tracts of the Armenian plateau are suitable only to nomads and their herds. Although the country's total land area once equaled that of England and Wales put together, Armenia has never supported a population of more than 4 million people.

Above: **Armenia is characterized by a mountainous landscape.**

Opposite: **The Khorvirap Monastery with the imposing Mount Ararat in the background.**

Armenia is situated in southwestern Asia. The country is bordered by Georgia and Azerbaijan to the north and east, Iran and the Azerbaijani province of Nakhichevan to the south, and Turkey to the west. At its greatest extent 2,000 years ago, the area occupied by the Armenian people amounted to well over 100,000 square miles (about 259,000 square km). Today Armenian territory covers only about 11,506 square miles (29,800 square km), making the country just slightly larger than the state of Maryland.

The main Armenian plateau lies at an average height of about 4,500–5,500 feet (1,372–1,676 m) above sea level. Armenia is higher than the countries that immediately surround it. Cut off from them on virtually all sides by barriers of lofty hills and mountain peaks, Armenia seems like a massive rockbound island rising out of the surrounding lowlands, steppes, and plains.

The geological structure of Armenia is unusually interesting, comprising elements from most phases of the earth's history.

GEOGRAPHIC FEATURES

Armenia is completely landlocked. However, neither the Black Sea to the west nor the Caspian Sea to the east is more than 300 miles (483 km) away.

Armenia's physical features range from heavily forested mountains to elevated plains that are bare of trees. The Lesser Caucasus Mountains line the country's northern, eastern, and western borders. The highest point of this range in Armenia, reaching 13,418 feet (4,090 m), is Mount Aragats, which is situated northwest of Armenia's capital, Yerevan.

Armenia is also crisscrossed by a number of rivers. Its largest body of water is Lake Sevan, which lies in the northeast.

The Ararat Plain lies in western Armenia, along Armenia's border with Turkey. It is Armenia's bread bowl. Although broken up by valleys and deep gorges, this long, narrow strip of land is heavily cultivated. The Ararat Plain is bisected by the Arax River, Armenia's longest river, which doubles as the country's border with Turkey to the west and with the Azerbaijani province of Nakhichevan and Iran to the south. The Arax River flows east, joining the Kura River in Azerbaijan and finally emptying into the Caspian Sea.

MOUNT ARARAT

Mount Ararat (Armenians also call it Mount Masis) is situated in what is now Turkey. However, Armenians once inhabited and ruled the Ararat area, and Mount Ararat, the legendary resting place of Noah's Ark, holds a special significance for Armenians.

The massif of Mount Ararat rises on its north and east sides. Out of the massif stand two peaks about seven miles (11 km) apart. Great Ararat is a huge broad-shouldered mass 16,945 feet (5,165 m) high, while Little Ararat is an elegant pyramidlike cone 12,877 feet (3,925 m) high.

There is a glacier on the northeast side of Great Ararat. The permanent snow line begins at the unusually high level of 14,000 feet (4,267 m). This is due to the small rainfall and the upward current of dry air from the plain of the Arax River. Both Great and Little Ararat consist of volcanic rocks.

ARMENIAN SOIL

Much of Armenia's soil is formed in part from the detritus of volcanic lava and is rich in nitrogen, potash, phosphates, and other useful chemicals. Typical soils encountered in Armenia are:

• the light brown alluvial earth of the Arax Valley and Ararat Plain. The soil in this region is rich in marl (a very fertile mix of calcium and clay usually formed in marine environments) but poor in humus (nutrients in the soil formed from decaying vegetable and animal matter) and has been irrigated, fertilized, and cultivated over many centuries.

• the rich brown soil of the drier hill country, where Armenians cultivate numerous kinds of crops ranging from corn to fruit and nut trees.

• the black mountain earth that accounts for a large portion of the Armenian uplands. This soil yields excellent crops of the hardier varieties of cereals and vegetables during the brief spring and summer seasons.

• the higher meadowlands covering the slopes of Armenia's great hill and mountain ranges. These rugged highland meadows yield little apart from hay and fodder for flocks and herds but play an important part in the country's economy by providing summer pasture for sheep and cattle.

LAKE SEVAN

Lake Sevan, one of the highest lakes in the world, is Armenia's largest body of water and accounts for 80 percent of the country's water resources. A long ridge of the Lesser Caucasus Mountains surrounds it.

Between 1930 and 1980, the level of water in the lake dropped significantly. The development of hydroelectric power stations downstream disturbed the ecological balance of the lake. Because of this, the volume of the lake was reduced by more than 40 percent. This drainage had

Lake Sevan is in danger from many fronts. Armenians have drawn water from it since 1930 under a plan to use its water for irrigation and hydroelectricity. By the early 1990s its level had dropped almost 20 feet (6 m). Cities and towns dispose of their organic wastes here, polluting its waters. Modern industries also use the lake as a dumping ground.

important effects on the fauna. The population of mammal and reptile species has declined, and the lake now sees only 50 species of migratory birds compared with 160 before the water level dropped. Steps have been taken to resolve this problem. Since 1982, water from the Arpa River has been carried into Lake Sevan through the Arpa-Sevan Tunnel, and this has increased the water level by 3.9 feet (1.2 m).

A view of the Arpa River, one of the main tributaries of the Arax River. The Arpa is 80 miles (129 km) long.

EARTHQUAKES

Earthquakes are a way of life in Armenia, as seismic disturbances occur frequently in this geologically active region. Many Armenian lives as well as buildings have been lost in earthquakes. Earthquakes in 1840 destroyed a village, a convent, and a chapel on Great Ararat, the legendary resting place of Noah's Ark.

The most devastating earthquake hit Armenia on the morning of December 7, 1988, killing approximately 25,000 people and causing severe property damage. The intensity of the earthquake virtually destroyed the towns of Spitak and Gyumri (formerly Leninakan), which lay near its epicenter.

The earthquake cut a swath through Armenia, crippling communications and transportation. Railroads were twisted or blocked. Traffic jams that lasted for hours made rescue work difficult. International rescue teams

and humanitarian organizations rushed to Armenia's aid. The December 1988 earthquake is still vivid in Armenians' memory.

A family makes a temporary shelter in a building damaged by the 1988 earthquake. Prefabricated buildings from Italy became home for many earthquake victims.

CLIMATE

Armenia is subjected to cold winters and hot summers, especially in the mountain and upland areas. The country experiences a wide variety of temperatures. In the winter, temperatures can fall to 40°F (-40°C) below freezing point. Armenians living in the north experience between 50 and 60 days of snowfall annually. In certain areas, the snow remains on the ground for up to seven months.

Summers are hot and dry, lasting from July to September. Temperatures range from 79°F (26°C) around Yerevan to 108°F (42°C) in other areas. Thunderstorms with strong winds but little rain are common, and summer often brings drought. A notable exception to these conditions is the Arax Valley, where winters are mild and the summer temperature averages about 90°F (32°F).

THE 1988 EARTHQUAKE

On December 7, 1988, an earthquake that registered between 7.5 and 8.5 on the Richter scale shook Armenia. Its epicenter was 15.5 miles (25 km) southeast of Gyumri. Although Armenia is earthquake-prone, this was the worst earthquake to hit the country in many years.

Medical teams soon arrived in Gyumri. The next day, soldiers also began to arrive in Spitak, one of the worst-hit towns, to begin rescue operations. About 1,500 wounded were evacuated by air. On December 8 the Soviet Union's then-prime minister, Nikolai Ryzhkov, flew into Yerevan from Moscow. Another Soviet leader, Mikhail Gorbachev, who was traveling in the United States, cut short his trip and flew to Armenia as well.

On December 9 the Armenian government announced that an estimated 700,000 Armenians were directly affected by the earthquake. Four-fifths of Gyumri was destroyed. All 11,000 apartment buildings in the city were damaged or destroyed, leaving thousands homeless. December 10 was declared a national day of mourning throughout the Soviet Union.

Thousands of people were brought out of the rubble and quickly evacuated, and by December 16 the death toll had risen to 23,286. Survivors dragged from the villages totaled 15,300. All together, 58 villages were destroyed, and 1,500 tremors had been reported at the epicenter since the big quake struck. The Armenian government estimated the worth of damage caused by the earthquake to be $5 billion. By December 18, 70,000 people had been evacuated from the earthquake area. Five hundred thousand people were officially homeless. The final death toll was 24,817 people. In Gyumri, food rationing was implemented.

The world community mobilized aid efforts. Forty countries set up disaster funds for earthquake victims. In the days following the earthquake, aid poured into Armenia from all over the world. The late businessman Armand Hammer donated $1 million and a planeload of medical equipment. Surgeons arrived with 10 tons (11 metric tons) of medical supplies. Airplanes arrived from Sweden, Syria, Bulgaria, Czechoslovakia, France, and the United States with supplies. The late Mother Teresa of Calcutta sent nurses to help in the earthquake disaster area. Almost 330 tons (363 metric tons) of food were arriving into Armenia every day. British aid funds totaled $1.3 million, while Soviet firms donated the proceeds of one voluntary working day to the earthquake victims. A son and a grandson of then-U.S. president George Bush visited Spitak and Yerevan, bringing 40 tons (44 metric tons) of aid with them. The amount of aid that poured into Armenia totaled $17 million.

Climatically the most agreeable areas of Armenia are those of the Ararat Plain to the southwest and the wooded mountains and hills in the north, where trees give shade in summer as well as protection from winter gales.

Rainfall occurs throughout the year, but most of Armenia's precipitation occurs in early winter with snow and in late spring with rain. Armenia receives an average of 15 inches (38 cm) of precipitation annually.

NOAH'S ARK

In the biblical story of Noah, the ark was a large vessel that saved Noah's family and pairs of all living creatures at the time of the Great Flood. Genesis 6:14-16 describes this floating houseboat. It was made of "gopher" wood, had three decks, and was 450 by 75 by 45 feet (137 by 23 by 14 m) in size. The Sumerian-Babylonian epic of the legendary King Gilgamesh gives a similar but more detailed account of an ark and a flood. Recent attempts to identify the ark's location at Mount Ararat have been dismissed as pseudoscientific and inconclusive. The most sensational evidence, a large wooden structure found in northeast Turkey, has been dated as only 1,200 years old.

Mount Ararat lies in the northeast corner of Turkey, near the border of Armenia. It is the traditional resting place of Noah's Ark. The summit of Mount Ararat is 16,945 feet (5,165 m) above sea level. Ararat is a dormant volcano, and its last eruption was on June 2, 1840.

Poppies grow wild in the steppes of Armenia.

FLORA

The flora of Armenia is as varied as its climate and its landscape. Forests cover only about one-tenth of the country.

Oak, beech, and hornbeam trees are very common in Armenia. Lime, ash, and maple trees are plentiful as well. The woods of Armenia also contain the plane tree, the yew, the walnut, and the hawthorn. Small forests of pine and spruce can be found in the northern regions of the country. Birch woods mixed with barberry, wild currant, wild rose, and mountain ash can be found as well.

Armenia is rich in fruits. Apricots are found in abundance. Other fruits include cherries, wild pears, crabapples, damsons, medlars, raspberries, dewberries, and more than 40 types of grapes.

The Arax Valley favors subtropical plants such as cotton, tobacco, olive, oleander, and mulberry. The peaks are mainly covered with steppe grasses—which are well suited to dry conditions—and with thorny, shrublike milk vetches. Between 4,000 and 6,000 feet (1,219–1,829 m) above sea level, wild rye and several other grasses flourish. Above 7,000 feet (2,134 m), the ground is often stony, and vegetation is sparse.

FAUNA

Armenia has a wide range of animal life—about 10,000 kinds of insects; more than 1,000 types of invertebrate creatures; and numerous vertebrates including 76 species of mammals, 349 species of birds, 44 varieties of reptiles, six sorts of amphibious animals, and 24 species of fish.

The mammals include moles and hedgehogs, bats, and various beasts of prey such as leopards, panthers, porcupines, hyenas, polecats, and wildcats. There is also a vast range of domesticated animals ranging from horses to rabbits.

Once a hunter's paradise, Armenia now boasts of the occasional wild boar, mountain goat, mouflon, and mottled deer. Wolves and jackals are also fairly common,

Bears used to be a common sight in Armenia, but their population has dwindled much in recent years due to hunting and the reduction of their habitat.

and there are a few species of bears and badgers. On open lands in the remote districts of the south, wild sheep are found. Fur-bearing animals include the squirrel, the otter, the fox, and the coypu. Also known as the nutria, the coypu is a rodent that has a reddish brown or yellowish brown outer coat, a dark gray undercoat, webbed hind feet, and strong teeth. Coypus grow to a length of 17–25 inches (43–64 cm) and have long scaly tails. They live in burrows in swampy areas, subsisting chiefly on freshwater plants. The undercoat is processed by furriers to resemble the beaver's pelt.

The marten is another creature valued for its fur. Martens are carnivorous mammals widely distributed throughout the Northern Hemisphere. They are long and graceful animals with short legs and toes and are armed with sharp claws. Martens live in hollows of trees when they are not in search of the rodents, birds, and birds' eggs that

A fox cub ventures out from its hole. Foxes are indigenous to Armenia.

constitute their food. Martens belong to the family *Mustelidae*, which includes weasels and skunks.

Among freshwater fish, the most notable are the *ishkhan*, or salmon trout, of Lake Sevan. Also found are whitefish, carp, and barbel.

Bird life in the country is varied and includes the raven, the crow, the vulture, the hawk, the falcon, the owl, the Caucasian grouse, the quail, the snipe, and the rare *ular* (mountain turkey). The pigeon and the dove are common, and there are plenty of waterfowl such as the coot and diverse species of duck.

Partridge is a common name applied to birds of the pheasant family, whose members have plump bodies, short tails, and short beaks adapted for picking up seeds. Their rounded wings and robust breast muscles power their explosive takeoffs to escape predators. They prefer to run, and they fly only short distances. Their habitats vary from rocky mountain slopes to forest floors. A few perch in trees. They are native to Armenia and other countries in Europe, Asia, North Africa, and the Middle East. The gray partridge of Europe, known to hunters as the Hungarian partridge, thrives especially in the grain fields. The chukar, another native species, is pale brownish gray, with bold black and white stripes on the flanks, a white throat bordered in black, and a bright red bill and feet. These birds are about 12–14 inches (30–36 cm) long.

CITIES

Armenia has a number of well-known cities, both ancient and modern. Yerevan (also known as Erevan), the capital and largest city of Armenia, is situated along the Hrazdan River, not very far from Armenia's border with Turkey. In the 1950s archaeologists unearthed a stone slab revealing that the city was founded in 782 B.C. by the Urartian king Argishti I and named Erebouni. Yerevan's location on the border between the Turkish and Persian empires meant that it was subjected to sieges. Many of Yerevan's old buildings were destroyed when these empires clashed. The city's modern and restored buildings are in traditional Armenian style.

Yerevan is situated in a scenic region noted for its orchards and vineyards. It is also an industrial, transportation, communications,

An overview of a part of Yerevan, with the Opera Building in the foreground.

and cultural center, populated by about 1.2 million people. As Armenia's capital and administrative and governmental center, Yerevan is not part of a province but is one in its own right.

As the center of Armenian culture, Yerevan is home to an opera house, a historical museum, and a music conservatory. The Yerevan State University (built in 1920); the Armenian Academy of Sciences; the National Archives; the Matenadaran, or the National

Yerevan's sports complex, where Armenia's Olympics contenders train for competition.

Manuscript Library, which houses the largest number of Armenian manuscripts in the world; and several technical institutes are situated in the city as well.

The Saint Gregory the Illuminator Cathedral, where the holy remains of Saint Gregory are kept, is also in Yerevan. In September 2001 the mostly Christian Armenian population celebrated the 1,700th anniversary of Armenia's acceptance of Christianity in the cathedral.

Another large city with an ancient history is Gyumri. Its name was changed to Alexandrapol in 1837 and to Leninakan, in honor of Lenin, in 1924. After the breaking up of the Soviet Union, it was renamed Gyumri. Modern Gyumri is an important industrial town of 150,000 inhabitants.

The third largest city in Armenia is Vanadzor (formerly Kirovakan), north of Yerevan.

The middle Arax Valley has a number of ancient sites that served as the capital of Armenia during different periods of its long history. Chief among these are Armavir, which was important during the Urartian and Hellenistic periods, and Echmiadzin (also called Vagharshapat), which is about 12 miles (19 km) from Yerevan. Echmiadzin is home to the Supreme Catholicos of the Armenian Apostolic Church. The oldest Armenian domed church, the Cathedral of Echmiadzin, is considered a major monument in Christian architecture.

The predominantly Armenian inhabitants of Stepanakert—the capital city of Nagorno-Karabakh—have suffered many hardships due to the ongoing hostilities between Armenia and Azerbaijan for control of the region.

HISTORY

ARMENIAN HISTORY dates back 500,000 years to the Acheulean period, when hunting and gathering peoples crossed the land in pursuit of migrating herds. For a succession of centuries, Armenia was in constant warfare with invaders—Assyrians, Romans, Byzantines, Arabs, and Turks—all of whom greatly influenced Armenian culture and beliefs.

Ancient Armenia grew out of the Urartian kingdom, a confederation of local tribes formed during the ninth century B.C. It became one of the strongest kingdoms in the Near East. The Urartians produced and exported ceramic, stoneware, and metalware and built fortresses, temples, palaces, and other large public buildings. An Urartian irrigation canal is in use today in Yerevan.

The Urartians were invaded many times, first by the Scythians and the Cimmerians of the Black Sea region, then by the Persians. The area that is modern-day Armenia did not see peace for many years. Armenia was part of the Persian Empire until Alexander the Great conquered it, bringing the empire, and with it Armenia, under his control.

More than 1,500 years after Alexander's death, Armenia fell into the hands of the Ottoman Empire, which it remained a part of until the first quarter of the 20th century. In 1922 Armenia became a Soviet republic. The early 1990s was a time of political and economic reform for the Soviet Union, with many of the Soviet republics making bids for independence. Armenia regained its independence in 1991.

Above: **The splendid medieval monastery of Noravank, founded in the early 13th century, includes the Church of Saint Karapet, which was constructed in the 10th century.**

Opposite: **The Tsiranavor church in Ashtarak. It was built between the fifth and sixth centuries. Armenia's landscape is peppered with heritage treasures of old.**

URARTU

The Urartian empire predates the Kingdom of Armenia and existed from 860 B.C. to 585 B.C. At its height, the empire spanned about 200,000 square miles (518,000 square km), from Mesopotamia to the Caucasus Mountains. Today this area is part of the Republic of Armenia and the eastern part of Turkey.

There is some debate among scholars about the origins of the name *Urartu*. Some believe that it is a biblical reference to Mount Ararat, while others believe that the name was given by the Assyrians, the Urartians' closest rivals, to the south of their own land borders.

Urartu first emerged, as a group of small tribes and villages, around 1200 B.C. The first real documentation of Urartu's rise to power was the acknowledgment of its existence in the inscriptions of Assyrian king Aramu (reigned 860–843 B.C.). The kings of Urartu between the seventh and ninth centuries B.C. continued to expand and consolidate the empire. During the reign of King Argishti (785–760 B.C.) it became one of the most powerful kingdoms in the region, stretching from the Arax River to the shores of the Black Sea.

The seventh century B.C. saw the empire's influence consolidating, although there were some occasional lapses in control. Between 714 and 645 B.C. the empire enjoyed a reasonably prosperous period, and sustained growth and development were evident.

The Urartian empire's preeminence began to diminish around 650 B.C. as other newly emerging empires challenged it for dominance. These rivals included the Scythian and the Median empires, which invaded Urartu in the early sixth century B.C. By the end of 580 B.C. the Urartian empire was reduced to a ruling family in name only with little if any regional influence or ambition. Around this time, aided by the Median kingdom, Urartu's House of Aramu, with Sadauri III at its helm, was overthrown and replaced by the Armenian Orontid family. With new leadership, Urartu reestablished its independence and again became an important regional kingdom, from which the early Armenian empire was born.

The pagan temple of Garni dates back to the first century A.D. It was destroyed in an earthquake in 1679 and reconstructed during the Soviet period.

MEDIA

Media, land of the Medes, was an ancient country in western Asia corresponding to modern-day Azerbaijan and Kurdistan and some of the region of Kermanshah in northwestern Iran. The Medes were Indo-Europeans, related to the ancient Persians, who entered Iran after 1200 B.C. and came under Assyrian domination. They probably secured their freedom about 625 B.C., when their king, Cyaxares, unified the Median tribes. In 621 B.C. Cyaxares conquered the Persians in southwestern Iran. In the same year, he joined forces with Babylonia in a successful attack on the Assyrians that led to the eventual destruction of the Assyrian Empire. At its height, the Median kingdom included western Iran, northern Mesopotamia, and part of Anatolia. After the Medes were overthrown in 550 B.C. by the Persian conqueror Cyrus the Great, Media was a province in successive empires of the region.

PERSIAN AND GREEK RULE

In the sixth century B.C., the Urartian kingdom, after a brief rule under the Medes, fell to the Persians under Cyrus the Great. Persia ruled Armenia from the sixth to the fourth centuries B.C. During this period,

Tigran the Great (reigned 95–55 B.C.) brought the Armenian kingdom to its zenith, expanding its territory as far south as Palestine and as far east as the Caspian Sea.

Armenia was one of the satrapies, or provinces, of the Persian Empire, governed by satraps, or viceroys, of Armenia's royal Orontid family. Much of Persian culture and religion was absorbed by the Armenians during this period.

In the fourth century B.C., Persia was conquered by Alexander the Great of Macedonia. Armenian culture subsequently absorbed Greek influences. This was a period of great economic success. Armenian cities thrived due to their position at the crossroads of trade routes connecting the Mediterranean with China, India, and Central Asia.

After Alexander's death in 323 B.C., his generals split his empire into three kingdoms. Hellenistic rule over Armenia finally came to an end when a local general, Artaxias, declared himself king of Greater Armenia (the region of northern Armenia) and founded a dynasty in 189 B.C. Artaxias expanded his territory by defining the borders of his land and unifying the Armenians.

The Armenian kingdom reached its peak during the reign of Tigran the Great (95–55 B.C.). Under Tigran, Armenian territory stretched from the Caspian Sea to the Mediterranean and from the Caucasus Mountains (which included parts of modern Georgia and Azerbaijan) to Palestine. This brought the Armenians into conflict with the Roman Empire, and Tigran was forced into an alliance with Rome. Armenia became the focus of Roman and Parthian-Persian rivalry for the next 400 years.

In A.D. 301, King Tiridates (also known as Tradt) III proclaimed Christianity as the sole religion in Armenian, thus making Armenia the first Christian nation in the world.

ALEXANDER THE GREAT

Alexander the Great (356–323 B.C.) was born in Pella, the capital of Macedonia. His father was King Philip II of Macedonia, and his mother was Princess Olympias of Epirus. As a child, Alexander was taught the princely art of warfare as well as educated in philosophy, mathematics, and science. The Greek philosopher Aristotle was one of the prince's tutors.

In 336 B.C., King Philip II was assassinated. Alexander succeeded him and executed his father's alleged murderers along with those who opposed him. No stranger to war—at age 16 he had led an army in battle—Alexander began a Persian expedition to replenish his war-depleted wealth in 334 B.C. With 30,000 infantry and 5,000 cavalry composed of Macedonians and Greeks, he crossed the Dardanelles. At the Granicus (now Kocabas) River, near Troy, he defeated an army of Persian and Greek mercenaries. The states of Asia Minor soon submitted to him.

Alexander continued his journey southward toward Syria. In 333 B.C., at Issus in northeastern Syria, he defeated the great Persian army of King Darius III. Darius fled, abandoning his army and his family. Two years later, while crossing Mesopotamia to reach the Tigris River, Alexander met Darius again. In a battle on the plain of Gaugamela, Alexander emerged victorious, and once again Darius retreated, this time to Bactria. When Darius was killed by the satrap of Bactria in 330 B.C., Alexander achieved his ambition to become the ruler of the Persian Empire.

In 332 B.C., Alexander founded the city of Alexandria in Egypt. The city later became the literary, scientific, and commercial center of the Greek world. Alexander's domain stretched along and beyond the southern shores of the Caspian Sea, including modern Afghanistan, and northward toward modern Turkmenistan.

Still not satisfied with his conquests, Alexander crossed the Indus River into Punjab in 326 B.C. His army, however, refused to proceed with him. They sailed to the Persian Gulf and crossed the desert to Media instead. Insufficient food and water took its toll on the men. The tireless Alexander, meanwhile, gathered information on the Persian Gulf in preparation for even more conquests, but in 323 B.C., not long after his arrival in Babylon, he became ill and died.

One of history's military geniuses, Alexander was a brilliant strategist. His speed in traversing and conquering vast expanses of territory is unparalleled. He brought surveyors, engineers, scientists, and historians on his campaigns and left relatives and close friends entrenched in conquered domains before proceeding onward to his next goal. Alexander founded and named several cities Alexandria after himself. Many Greeks from his army settled in these cities, and the Greek influence grew as the use of their language and culture spread.

THE ADOPTION OF CHRISTIANITY

Christianity was introduced to Armenia by the apostles Thaddeus and Bartholomew in the first century A.D. In A.D. 301, Armenia embraced Christianity as the state religion, thus becoming the first nation to do so. Armenia's ruler, King Tiridates III, was converted to Christianity by Gregory Parthev (Gregory the Parthian). Parthev was named "the Illuminator" by the Armenians because he enlightened the ruler and the nation.

The Persian Empire's attempts to impose Zoroastrianism on the Christian Armenians met with great resistance. In A.D. 451, under the leadership of Vardan Mamikonian (a statue of whom graces Yerevan), Armenians faced the Persians in the Battle of Avarayr. Being heavily outnumbered, the Armenians were defeated, but guerrilla warfare continued in the mountainous regions.

Finally, under Vahan Mamikonian, Vardan's nephew, the Armenians convinced the Sasanians to restore their freedom of worship. Vahan gained this freedom after the death of the King Peroz in 484. Due to internal struggles, the Sasanians were not able to conquer Armenia, and in return for Vahan's support, King Vagharsh, Peroz's successor, granted Armenia freedom of religion.

In the latter part of the fourth century, much of Armenia was divided between Byzantine and Persian rulers. The Persians continued to fight for the remaining Armenian lands until the Arabs invaded the country in the seventh century.

THE ARAB AND SELJUK INVASIONS

Armenians lived under Arab control for more than 200 years, beginning in the seventh century A.D. Although there was formal religious tolerance for Christians and Jews at that time, many Armenians left for Byzantine-controlled western Armenia to avoid conversion to Islam, the religion brought by the Arab conquerors. The period under Arab rule saw a continuation in Armenian art, documentation, trade, and church and secular literature. History was documented by Moses of Khoren, John of Drashanakert, and Thomas Arzruni. The poetry and hymns of Gregory of Narek, many of which are still used in churches today, were recorded during this period.

The Armenian kingdom of Ani fell to the Byzantines in 1045 and to the Seljuks in 1064. The Battle of Manzikert in 1071 destroyed the Byzantine Imperial Army and prevented it from reconquering Armenia. This invasion forced a number of Armenians to move to the west to Cappadocia and later to the south toward the Taurus Mountains, close to the Mediterranean Sea. In 1080, under the leadership of Ruben, these Armenians founded the kingdom of Cilicia, which comprised the region of the plateau surrounding the central Taurus Mountains and the plain between the Taurus and Armanus mountains.

THE GOLDEN AGE OF ARMENIAN ILLUMINATION

This period of time in Cilicia is regarded as the golden age of Armenian illumination, as the kingdom enjoyed high culture and great prosperity even as the Armenian homeland was under occupation. The period from the 12th to the 14th centuries was a time of important cultural renaissance in northern Armenia.

Close contact with the Crusaders and other Europeans led the Cilicians to adopt Western European ideas and became a country of barons, knights, and serfs. The Cilicians even adopted the lavish decorations and contemporary paintings of the Europeans. Latin influence was strong in Cilicia due mainly to the great military expeditions of Holy Roman Emperor Frederick II (1194–1250) and King Louis IX of France (1215–70). Many Italian colonies were also established in Cilicia, and Armenian colonies were founded in Italy.

In the late 16th century, the Armenians fell under the control of the Ottoman Empire, a Muslim Turkish empire that had descended from the Seljuks. A small part of Armenia came under Persian rule.

OTTOMAN RULE

Under Ottoman rule, Armenians lost all vestiges of an independent political life. The Ottoman rulers advocated a policy of moving populations of Armenian regions to the Ottoman capital, pulling in the resources of skilled artisans and the merchant class.

Shah Abbas of Persia also figured prominently in the exodus of Armenians in the early 17th century. The shah, who had made peace with the Ottoman Empire in 1590, advanced in 1603 to retake Azerbaijan from the Turks. In the process, he moved some 300,000 Armenians to the south. In 1605 he resettled Armenian merchants and artisans from Julfa to his new capital, Isfahan.

During the last quarter of the 19th century, Ottoman Armenians agitated for change against discrimination, heavy taxation, and armed attacks. From 200,000 to 300,000 Armenians were massacred between 1894 and 1896.

During World War I (1914–18), the Turks began killing or driving away the entire Armenian population. The Ottoman government wanted to make room for Turkish and Kurdish settlers. Moreover, it believed that the Armenians were pro-Russian. Approximately 1.5 million Armenians died during this genocide.

At the end of World War I, after the rise of the Bolsheviks in Russia, an independent Republic of Armenia was declared within Russian Armenia in May 1918. However, external forces, especially pressure from the Turks, led to the collapse of the republic in 1920. The Soviet Red Army moved into the territory, and in 1922 Armenia was made a Soviet republic.

Above: **An engraving of Abbas I of Persia. Many Armenians escaped the conflict between the Ottoman Empire and Persia by migrating eastward to countries in Asia.**

Opposite (top): **Ottoman sultan Abdul Hamid II.** *(Bottom):* **The Sardapat War Memorial commemorates Armenia's 1918 battle with the Turkish army.**

THE ARMENIAN GENOCIDE

A bleak period in Armenian history stretches from the late 19th century to the early 20th century. This period was marked by the killing of 1.5 million Armenians by the Turks in 1915–16.

In the late 19th century, following the example of Europe, the Ottoman sultans decided to bring about progressive change to their empire under the banner of the Tanzimat, *tanzimat* (TAHN-zee-MAHT) being the Turkish word for "reorganization." Planned and begun under Mahmud II, the Tanzimat modernized the Ottoman Empire by extending the reach of government into all aspects of life, overshadowing the autonomous guilds that had monopolized most governmental functions prior to this. A modern administration and army were created along Western lines, with highly centralized bureaucracies. A secular system of education and justice was organized. Large-scale public works programs modernized the infrastructure of the empire, building cities, roads, railroads, and telegraph lines. New agricultural methods also contributed to the Ottoman revitalization. Taking advantage of this, Armenians in the eastern provinces of the Ottoman Empire began to promote the notion of an independent Armenian nation.

All reform movements were brought to an end during the reign of Sultan Abdul Hamid II (1876–1909) after the Russo-Turkish War of 1877–78, which signaled the decline of the Ottoman Empire in the Balkans and the Caucasus. Despite the number of Armenians who fought for the Ottoman Empire alongside the Turkish troops in the war of 1877–78, the Turks blamed their defeat on the Armenians, who were thought to be pro-Russian. This resulted in a series of massacres from 1894 to 1896.

Under the Young Turk regime of Enver Pasha, Talaat Pasha, and Ahmed Djemal Pasha, Turkish persecution of the Armenians continued during World War I, when they were killed or forced to relocate. Many died from heat and exhaustion during their arduous march through the Syrian, Mesopotamian, and Arabian deserts.

The Armenians commemorate the genocide on April 24 every year. It was on April 24, 1915, that all the Armenian intellectuals of Istanbul were rounded up by Turkish authorities and imprisoned or executed.

An old steam train with the Soviet insignia, a reminder that Armenia used to be a Soviet republic.

A SOVIET REPUBLIC

Armenia, Azerbaijan, and Georgia signed a treaty to form the Transcaucasian Soviet Federated Socialist Republic in March 1922. Despite promising to grant Armenia control of Nagorno-Karabakh and Nakhichevan, where a large population of Armenians resided, the Soviet Union placed the two regions under Azerbaijani governance in 1923. In 1936 the Transcaucasian federation was abolished, and Armenia as well as Azerbaijan and Georgia became separate constituent republics of the Soviet Union.

The first priority of the Soviet regime was to neutralize nationalist forces in Armenia. This was accomplished by banning the political group Dashnaktsuyun (Armenian Revolutionary Federation) in November 1923. The members of Dashnaktsuyun were politically active in seeking an independent Armenia. In addition, persecution of the church began in the 1920s, as places of worship and religious presses were closed. The "Russification" of Armenia not only ended the practicing of age-old rural beliefs but also led to the attempt to destroy Armenian literature and culture. The works of many prominent Armenian writers, such as Raffi (Akop Melik-Akopian), were destroyed or banned during this period. Armenian literature and culture, however, continued to thrive in the Soviet period and continue to this day.

The breakup of the Soviet Union beginning in the 1980s led to Armenia's second attempt to gain independence. In 1990 the Armenian National Movement won a majority of seats in parliament and formed a government. On September 21, 1991, the Armenian people voted overwhelmingly in favor of independence in a national referendum, and an independent Armenia came into being.

THE STRUGGLE FOR NAGORNO-KARABAKH

Nagorno-Karabakh was at one time a state in its own right. About 80 percent of its population of approximately 180,000 people are Armenians. In 1921 the Caucasian section of the Russian Communist Party declared the country part of Armenia. This decision was reversed a few days later by the commissioner for nationalities, Joseph Stalin, who placed it under Azerbaijani control.

A woman weeps over the grave of her son, a casualty of the conflict over Nagorno-Karabakh, as her husband serenades him. Today the region of Nagorno-Karabakh is an independent entity known as the Mountainous Republic of Karabagh, though it is recognized only by the Republic of Armenia. It is also important to note that Armenia and Karabagh are separate political entities.

The pogroms against the Armenians in Azerbaijan started in Sumgait, Azerbaijan. The pressure to unify Nagorno-Karabakh with Armenia started in 1988 with demonstrations in Yerevan and elsewhere against Azerbaijani repression of the Armenians in Nagorno-Karabakh. This resulted in a series of killings of Armenians in Azerbaijan. Moscow intervened by imposing direct rule over Nagorno-Karabakh. The protests continued.

Russia returned control of Nagorno-Karabakh to Azerbaijan in November 1989. Armenia protested and declared Nagorno-Karabakh part of the Armenian republic. After renewed ethnic violence in Azerbaijan, Soviet troops stormed in, and a state of emergency was established that lasted until August 1991.

Azerbaijan and Armenia became independent in 1991. After the last Soviet troops left Nagorno-Karabakh in early 1992, the conflict turned into a full-scale war. In May 1994, under the Minsk Group, which is responsible for assisting negotiations to end the conflict between the two countries, the two sides agreed to a ceasefire. Although the United Nations Security Council has put a lot of pressure on the countries, their differences have generally remained unresolved.

GOVERNMENT

ARMENIA REMAINED A PART OF the Ottoman Empire for nearly 400 years—from the late 16th century to the early 20th century. Toward the latter part of the 19th century, human-rights violations against the Christian Armenians by the Turkish authorities intensified Armenian nationalist sentiment, which was already aroused by nationalist literature. Nationalist parties—the Dashnak and the Hnchak—worked to bring "the Armenian question" onto the international agenda. European authorities expressed concern about the Armenian situation but did little when hundreds of thousands of Armenians were massacred between 1894 and 1896.

Above: **The federal building in the capital city of Yerevan houses government ministries.**

Opposite: **An Armenian election official empties a ballot box for counting in the presidential election of 2003. See-through ballot boxes were used to ensure that every possibility of fraud was eliminated.**

During World War I, the Turkish authorities, considering the Christian Armenians sympathetic to their Russian foes, embarked on a program of forced deportations and massacres. This resulted in the death of roughly 1.5 million Armenians and has been called the first genocide of modern times. Thousands of Armenians migrated to Russian Armenia.

The Russians were galvanized into taking action. In 1918 an independent Republic of Armenia was formed under the Dashnaks. For two years the Dashnak administration struggled with the republic's economic problems while fending off attacks from the Turks and fighting for international recognition. In December 1920 the Dashnaks turned over the administration to the Communists, and the Soviet Republic of Armenia was formed in 1922.

Armenia declared its independence on August 23, 1991, and withdrew from the Soviet Union in September 1991. Since then, much of the government's work has been focused on Armenia's dispute with

The eagle, a symbol of the people who populated Armenia before the creation of Urartu, is a popular motif in Armenia. It symbolizes the might and heroism of Armenians.

Azerbaijan over Nagorno-Karabakh. The first president of the republic was Levon Ter-Petrosyan.

THE POLITICAL SYSTEM

Armenia is a republic with a presidential governing system. The country's official name is Hayastani Hanrapetut'yun, or Republic of Armenia. From 1990 to 1995, the political, legal, social, and economic relationships of the previous political system were slowly dismantled.

The political life of the country changed on July 5, 1995, when Armenians voted to adopt the constitution of the Republic of Armenia. The constitution provides legal guarantees of civil rights, the development of democratic institutions, and the creation of a market economy to secure the future stability of the state.

A mass meeting of the opposition in Yerevan in 1996.

ROBERT S. KOCHARIAN, PRESIDENT OF ARMENIA

Robert Kocharian (*pictured below*) was elected president of Armenia in 1998 and reelected in 2003. He was born in 1954 in Stepanakert in Nagorno-Karabakh and received his early education there.

Between 1972 and 1974 he served in the Soviet army. He began his professional career as an engineer in Stepanakert. His political career started in the 1980s when he held various positions in Nagorno-Karabakh's Communist groups. Kocharian founded and headed the Miatsum organization, which campaigned to reunite Nagorno-Karabakh with Armenia. Other milestones in his political career include:

1989–90s
Deputy of Armenia's Supreme Soviet,
the country's highest legislative body, and
member of the Presidium of the Supreme Soviet

1991
Deputy of the Nagorno-Karabakh Republic's
Supreme Soviet of the first convocation

1992
Chairman of the State Defense Committee and
prime minister of Nagorno-Karabakh

1994
President of the Nagorno-Karabakh Republic

1997
Prime Minister of the Republic of Armenia

1998
President of the Republic of Armenia

2003
Reelected as president of the Republic of Armenia

As president, Robert Kocharian continues to negotiate a peaceful resolution on the status of Nagorno-Karabakh. He held talks with Azerbaijan president Ilham Aliyev in 2004 and 2006 on the future of the region and the fundamental principles of a settlement to the conflict. However, there has still been no resolution.

The president oversees the normal activity of the executive, legislative, and judicial authorities. The same person cannot hold the office of president for more than two consecutive terms.

ARMENIA'S DECLARATION OF INDEPENDENCE

The rights of the citizens of the Republic of Armenia are encompassed in its declaration of independence. There are 12 main points in the declaration:

1. The Armenian Soviet Socialist Republic is renamed the Republic of Armenia and has its own flag, coat of arms, and anthem.

2. The Republic of Armenia is a self-governing state, with the power to act independently of other states. Only the constitution and laws of the Republic of Armenia are valid for the whole territory.

3. The people of the republic exercise the authority of their state directly and through representative bodies on the basis of the constitution and laws of the republic. The Supreme Council speaks on their behalf.

4. Residents of Armenia are granted citizenship of Armenia. Armenians of the diaspora also have the right of this citizenship. Armenia guarantees the free and equal development of its citizens regardless of national origin, race, or creed.

5. To guarantee the security of the country and the inviolability of its borders, the republic creates its own armed forces, internal troops, and organs of state and public security. Armenia has its share of the Soviet Union's military apparatus but determines the regulation of military service for its citizens independently. Military units and military bases or buildings of other countries can be located in Armenia only if permitted by Armenia's Supreme Council. The armed forces of the Republic of Armenia can be deployed only by a decision of its Supreme Council.

6. Armenia conducts an independent foreign policy. It establishes direct relations with other states and national-state units of the former Soviet Union and participates in the activity of international organizations.

7. The national wealth of the Republic of Armenia—the land, the earth's crust, the airspace, the water, and other natural resources, as well as economic, intellectual, and cultural capabilities—are the property of its people. Their regulation, usage, and possession are determined by the laws of the republic. The republic has the right to its share of the national wealth of the Soviet Union.

8. The Republic of Armenia determines the principles and regulations of its economic system. It creates its own money, national bank, and financial and tax systems based on multiple forms of property ownership.

9. Within its territory, the Republic of Armenia guarantees freedom of speech, press, and conscience; separation of legislative, executive, and judicial powers; a multiparty system; equality of political parties under the law; and depoliticization of law-enforcement bodies and armed forces.

10. Armenian is the state language in all spheres of the republic's life. The republic creates its own system of education and of scientific and cultural development.

11. The Republic of Armenia wants to achieve international recognition of the 1915 genocide in Ottoman Turkey and Western Armenia.

12. Until a new constitution is approved, this declaration is the basis for the introduction of amendments to the current constitution.

Armenia's coat of arms features an eagle and a lion holding a shield. The imposing Mount Ararat—with Noah's Ark on it—lies in the heart of the shield, surrounded by a double-headed eagle, scepter-bearing lions, and two doves. Below the shield are the hilt of a sword, a stylized branch, a sheaf of wheat, and the links of a broken chain.

GOVERNMENT LEADERS

The government is headed by the president, who appoints a prime minister to oversee the duties of the executive branch. The prime minister, in turn, is responsible for recommending members of the Supreme Council, who are then officially appointed by the president.

THE NATIONAL ASSEMBLY

The National Assembly implements Armenia's legislative, or lawmaking, powers. This body carries out its activities through sessions, permanent and temporary committees, and deputies. It is a single-chamber representative body, and its members are elected by a group of single-member districts of equal representation.

Republic Square in Yerevan. In the background are the Armenian History Museum and National Art Gallery.

ANDRANIK MARKARYAN

Andranik Markaryan was born in 1951. He graduated from Yerevan Polytechnic Institute's Technical Cybernetics Department and is a qualified computer engineer. He was appointed prime minister of Armenia in May 2000, replacing Aram Sarkissian.

He was involved in politics since 1965. His early political career included membership in the National United Party, which operated when Armenia was part of the Soviet Union. He was against the Soviet totalitarian system and campaigned for a democratic and independent Armenian state.

He became a member of the Republican Party of Armenia in 1992, rising to become the chairman of the party's board for three consecutive terms, beginning in 1993. Between 1995 and 1999 he was a member of the first convention of the National Assembly, and he remained a member of the National Assembly from 1999. After the 2004 elections, he remained in office and headed the coalition government formed as a result of the elections.

Markaryan died of heart failure on March 25, 2007.

Members of the National Assembly are elected to serve a four-year term. The first parliamentary elections were held in July 1995. At that time, the law allowed for 190 deputies. However, in the same year the Constitution of the Republic of Armenia lowered the number of parliamentary seats from 190 to 131.

The National Assembly is held twice a year. The president of the republic or the chairman of the National Assembly can call extraordinary sessions at the initiative of the government or a minimum of one-third of the total number of deputies.

THE JUDICIAL BRANCH AND THE CONSTITUTIONAL COURT

Armenia's judicial system underwent a reorganization in 1999. The courts have the general power, or jurisdiction, to hear all civil and criminal matters. There are three types of courts: the first-level courts, or district courts; the courts of appeal; and the courts of review. There is a separately appointed Judicial Council that oversees the independence of all judicial bodies and is headed by the president of the republic. The justice minister and the chief prosecutor hold the vice president positions on the council. There are 14 other members of the Judicial Council, who are appointed by the president. The Judicial Council plays a prominent role in the judiciary of the country, as it has authority over the entire judicial system. It is a creation of a separate act of parliament and has the authority to appoint, dismiss, and discipline judges.

A traffic police officer issuing a ticket to a motorist. To appeal the ticket, the motorist would have to take the case to district court.

Armenians casting their ballots during the country's presidential elections in February 2003.

A separately created Constitutional Court rules on matters relating to conformity or compliance with the country's constitution. It consists of nine members, four of whom are appointed by the president and the remaining five by the National Assembly. It also approves international agreements and determines election-related questions. However, matters to be heard by the Constitutional Court must be proposed by the president and approved by a two-thirds majority of the National Assembly. In addition, election-related issues can be brought only by a candidate who ran for parliament or president.

There is no military court system, and military matters are heard in the civil courts, though they are handled by a military prosecutor specializing in the field.

Trials are held in public except when government or national secrets are involved. Juries are not used, and decisions are passed by single judges, except in the courts of appeal and review, which are presided over by a panel of judges.

Making sure all is in place for the guard of honor for a visiting head of state.

DEFENSE

Following the breakup of the Soviet Union in 1991, Armenia became a member of the Commonwealth of Independent States (CIS). Armenia participates in the CIS collective security system, but it has also established its own armed forces, estimated to have 60,000 troops in 2002. There is, in addition, a paramilitary force attached to the Ministry of Internal Affairs. In 2003 the country's draft budget allocated $82 million for defense.

Armenia joined the North Atlantic Treaty Organization (NATO) Partnership for Peace program of military cooperation in 1994.

FOREIGN RELATIONS

Since 1991 the Armenian government has moved quickly and effectively to establish friendly and close diplomatic and economic ties with the outside world. More than 120 countries have formally recognized Armenia, and more than 70 have officially established diplomatic relations.

Thirty countries have opened embassies in Armenia, including the United States, Russia, Belgium, China, Egypt, France, Georgia, Germany, Greece, India, Italy, Iran, Canada, and the United Kingdom. On its part, Armenia has secured a permanent presence in more than 60 countries worldwide, opening embassies and missions. These include Austria, Belarus, Brazil, Canada, Croatia, Cuba, Egypt, Georgia, Hungary, Israel, Republic of Korea, Morocco, Norway, Romania, Sweden, Spain, Ukraine, the United Arab Emirates, the United States, and the United Kingdom.

Armenia has also become an active participant in global issues and concerns. It is a member of more than 35 international organizations including the United Nations, the Council of Europe, the Commonwealth of Independent States, the Organization for Security and Cooperation in Europe, NATO's Partnership for Peace, the North Atlantic Cooperation Council, the International Monetary Fund (IMF), the International Bank for Reconstruction and Development, and the World Trade Organization (WTO). It is also an observer member of the Eurasian Economic Community, La Francophonie, and the Non-Aligned Movement.

Since 1991 the U.S. and Armenian governments have gradually expanded relations. In addition to joining the WTO, Armenia was granted permanent normal trade relations status with the United States in 2004.

The Commonwealth of Independent States, or CIS, is an association of 11 former Soviet republics. It was established on December 8, 1991. The members are Armenia, Georgia, Russia, Ukraine, Belarus, Kazakhstan, Kyrgyzstan, Tajikistan, Uzbekistan, Azerbaijan, and Moldova. Turkmenistan discontinued as a permanent member in 2005 and is now an associate member. CIS members cooperate in economic and defense matters.

Armenia's humanitarian officials.

ECONOMY

IN THE 1980S AND 1990S, ARMENIA's economy was plagued by natural and human-caused disasters. A severe earthquake in 1988 caused massive destruction to its infrastructure. Its involvement in a prolonged war in Nagorno-Karabakh and the closure of the Azeri and Turkish borders blocked the country of its main trade routes.

Despite the setbacks, a radical IMF-sponsored reform program implemented in 1994 helped to boost the country's ravaged economy. One of these reforms was the privatization of large and midsize enterprises. These swift changes helped restart the country's economy. Between 1994 and 2000, the economy grew at an average yearly rate of 5.5 percent. In 2001 the government took steps to continue improving the business environment, promoting exports of Armenian goods and increasing

Left: **A shepherd tending his sheep.**

Opposite: **Currency exchange rates displayed in a street in the city of Yerevan.**

private-sector investment. A plan was put into place to improve and shorten the time for registering and receiving licenses for businesses. These measures helped businesses grow and promoted investment. The result was an improved economy—in 2004 Armenia's economy grew by 10 percent, and in 2006 it grew by 13.4 percent with a per capita income of about $5,700.

Armenia has a varied economy. Construction, industry, agriculture, and services are the major sectors supporting growth.

LABOR AND EMPLOYMENT

Although poverty is still high in Armenia, government measures plus a strong economic performance in recent years have helped reduce poverty in the country.

The official unemployment rate fell from 10 percent in 2003 to 7.4 percent in 2006. However, unofficial estimates put unemployment figures at close to 30 percent.

Despite the government's attempts to strengthen the business regulatory environment, the economy faces many structural bottlenecks. The lack of employment opportunities has resulted in a substantial emigration of workers. A new labor code was passed by the National Assembly in November 2004 to help alleviate this problem.

There were about 1.2 million employed Armenians in the country by 2006, with the majority of the workforce employed in the agriculture (45 percent) and services (30 percent) sectors.

AGRICULTURE

In the agricultural areas, which include the fertile Arax Valley, Armenians grow vegetables, fruits (especially grapes), and tobacco, among other

crops. Agricultural products include specialty teas and oils such as geranium, rose, and peppermint.

As local food production does not satisfy domestic needs, the country imports large quantities of food. During the Soviet period, Armenia imported almost two-thirds of its bread and dairy products from other Soviet republics. The economic blockade by Azerbaijan and the civil war in Georgia caused food supplies to diminish. In the early 1990s, however, in contrast to industrial production, agricultural output increased considerably. Agriculture plays an important part in the country's overall economy. It contributes about a fifth of the total national income, and almost half of the country's workers are employed in this industry.

INDUSTRY

The industrial sector in Armenia is made up of machine building, instrument making, radio electronics, chemical industry, construction

A woman takes a break from her work in a vineyard. While Armenia is well known for its wines among the former Soviet republics, the rest of the world is just beginning to have access to them.

Before independence, Armenia's tobacco was exported solely to the Soviet bloc. Since independence, however, Armenia has been looking to expand its export market for tobacco.

TOBACCO

Tobacco comes from the genus *Nicotiana*. As its name suggests, nicotine, an addictive substance, is found in this species, concentrated in its leaves. The leaves, once cured, are used for smoking (in cigarettes, cigars, and pipes), for chewing, as snuff, and for the extraction of nicotine, which is an ingredient of products such as insecticides. The common tobacco plant is usually cultivated to a height of about 3–4 feet (1–1.2 m), although if left unpruned it can grow as high as 10 feet (3 m). Its leaves branch out from a central stem to a length ranging from 3 inches (8 cm) in some varieties to 3 feet (1 m) in others.

Armenia is one of many countries with soil and climatic conditions suitable for tobacco cultivation. Even then, the growth process is labor intensive, and a great deal of care goes into producing quality tobacco. Each tobacco variety has its own moisture and fertilizing requirements. Seedlings are germinated in boxes before being transplanted to the field. Tobacco plants grown for the fine thin leaves used to wrap around cigars must be cultivated under a cloth canopy. Harvesting by hand occurs in stages. Harvested leaves are dried and then cured by air, fire, or heat. The method used affects the aroma and flavor of the tobacco.

After curing, the leaves are graded by factors such as color, size, and their position on the main stem; lower leaves have less nicotine. The different grades of leaves are packed in bales and shipped to tobacco warehouses for auction.

materials industry, precious metals and stones processing, light industry, and consumer goods.

Armenia's wide-ranging manufacturing industries produce metal-cutting machine tools, forging and pressing machines, electric motors, tires, knitwear, shoes, silk fabric, chemicals, trucks, watches, industrial tools, and mainframe computers. The country's well-developed light industry sector focuses on textiles, clothing, and carpets and exports to the United States and Western Europe.

Armenia also produces several types of consumer durable goods such as radios, washing machines, freezers, refrigerators, and bicycles. However, Armenia's production of the more popular consumer durables—such as television sets, stereos, vacuum cleaners, and furniture—does not meet domestic demand.

When under Soviet rule, Armenia was an important center for scientific research. It still produces computers, calculators, measuring instruments, and semiconductor-related items.

Brandy and other liqueurs are among Armenia's export products.

MINING AND ENERGY

Armenia has a fairly healthy cache of mineral resources, including marble, basalt, granite, tufa, lead, zinc, gold, copper, and silver. Iron ore is also mined. Mineral products include soda. The country is a major source of molybdenum, aluminum, and rare metals such as selenium and tellurium. Armenia is also a producer of mineral water.

Although it has not been proven, studies indicate that Armenia has reserves of about six billion barrels of oil and six trillion cubic feet

Vanadzor's central heating plant, powered by nuclear energy.

(20 billion cubic meters) of natural gas. In addition, it is estimated that there are 100 million tons of coal in the country.

The country is highly dependent on energy supplies from Russia and Turkmenistan. The production of energy fell sharply after the 1986 Chernobyl disaster and the 1988 earthquake. The situation became critical in 1991 when Azerbaijan closed off the main pipeline transporting Russian gas to Armenia. At the moment, a secondary pipeline running through Georgia is the only external source of gas for the country.

Severe shortages have forced the Armenian government to seek alternative energy sources. In 2001 the governments of Iran and Armenia signed an agreement to build an 88-mile (142-km) gas pipeline between the two countries. With the pipeline launched for use in 2007, Armenia receives more than 396 million gallons (1.5 million cubic m) of gas from Iran each day.

TRANSPORTATION AND COMMUNICATION

Armenia has about 520 miles (837 km) of railroad with links to Turkey, Iran, Georgia, and Russia. The main highway to Georgia passes through Azerbaijan, while the reconstruction of a bridge over the Arax River has improved road access to Iran, facilitating the supply of consumer goods.

Armenia is the only Transcaucasian republic to operate a nuclear power plant. The plant is located in Metsamor, a town about 23 miles (37 km) from the city of Yerevan.

There is also an airport that links the country with the rest of the world. The nearest seaport is Poti in Georgia, through which Armenia gets access to the countries of the Black Sea region.

The telecommunications network in Armenia is still undergoing development. There were approximately 20 telephones for every 100 people in 2004. Telephone services, both fixed and mobile, are offered by private companies. Internet service is also available, though access is mostly via dial-up. At the end of 2004, there were only 65 Internet users out of every 1,000 people. In 2005 there were about 150,000 people with access to the Internet.

Transportation in Yerevan includes trains, buses, and taxis.

ENVIRONMENT

LIKE THE OTHER CAUCASIAN COUNTRIES, Armenia faces many environmental cleanup issues, some of which are legacies of the former Soviet Union. After its independence, Armenia's ongoing conflict with Azerbaijan and the country's economic growth threatened the balance of its ecosystem, affecting both plant and animal habitats.

HABITAT LOSS

Many bird species in Armenia are now on the endangered species list, and the recorded number of migratory birds has dropped significantly from 160 to only 50 species. There has also been a drop in the number of reptiles from semidesert areas, including the spur-thighed tortoise, the toadhead agama, the golden grass mabuya, the Caucasian sand boa, the Montpellier snake, the racerunner, and the snake-eyed lizard

Left: **The landscape near Goris. The country is trying to strike a balance between urban development and ecological conservation.**

Opposite: **An aerial view of air pollution over Yerevan at sunset.**

Sheep grazing on one of the diminishing grasslands of Armenia.

from the Arax Valley. An important population of a common subspecies of racerunner has nearly disappeared from the Sevan basin because of agricultural land use.

Lake Sevan's declining water level has also had major repercussions on several wetland habitats in the area. Many marshland species of lizards, waders, and mammals have disappeared from that area.

DEFORESTATION

In the 1980s and 1990s Armenians were faced with hardships due to several factors—a massive earthquake, the armed conflict in Nagorno-Karabakh, and the energy blockade imposed by Azerbaijan. These were difficult obstacles to overcome. Lack of fuel and the need to survive the cold winter drove Armenians to begin cutting down trees. As Armenia's economy improved, urbanization, construction, and road building contributed to deforestation.

About 17,657,333 cubic feet (500,000 cubic m) of wood are burned in Armenia every year for fuel. This means more than 9,884 acres (4,000 ha) of forests are cut for fuel as well as for other commercial or developmental purposes. Since the turn of the 19th century, Armenia has witnessed a dramatic fall in forest cover from 25 percent of its territory to the current low, an estimated 8-9 percent.

Deforestation has created many problems and hurt Armenia both socially and economically. Deforestation can lead not only to the extinction of many animal and plant species but also to topsoil erosion, flooding, and landslides.

The sparse forest cover in southern Armenia.

A deforested area—the result of the widespread felling of trees for fuel during the economic blockade by Azerbaijan —in the outskirts of the city of Yerevan.

The government has implemented several measures to help reduce deforestation. Laws have been introduced banning commercial clearance of forests. Proper use and protection of forests have also been regulated, and various nongovernment organizations have become actively involved in restoring deforested areas.

SOIL POLLUTION

More than 40 percent of Armenia's soil is exposed to erosion. This erosion is caused by a combination of natural and artificial factors such as deforestation, earthquakes, and industrial activities such as mining and mineral processing.

A significant portion of the land that has suffered from degradation was once used for agricultural purposes. Chemical fertilizers, herbicides, and pesticides, especially chlorine-organic compounds that remain in the soil for 15-20 years, have long been used in Armenia.

Mining and other metallurgy enterprises pollute the soil with heavy metals and chemical compounds, and the volume of accumulated industrial wastes reaches several hundred million cubic meters.

NUCLEAR POWER PLANT

There is one nuclear power plant in Armenia, in the town of Metsamor. The nuclear plant generates about 40 percent of the country's electricity. Although the plant suffered no physical damage in the 1988 earthquake, it was shut down in response to domestic and international concern about its safety.

With loans from Russia and safety assistance from the United States and the International Atomic Energy Agency, one of the plant's two reactor units was reopened in 1996. The plant will run until the end of its 30-year service life in 2016.

Lermontovo in Armenia, an example of Armenians' coexistence with their natural surroundings.

View of part of Armenia's vegetation and scenic hills near Garni. Armenia's vast expanse of vegetation is also not spared from the threat of deforestation.

Armenia has two known nuclear research facilities—the Yerevan Physics Institute and the Analitsark Plant in Gyumri.

ALTERNATIVE ENERGY

Armenia also sources energy from thermal power plants, which use a combination of oil and natural gas, and hydropower. These two alternative sources produce 60 percent of the country's energy.

With increasing pressure from environmentalists and concerned international government agencies, Armenia is looking at a cleaner and more environmentally friendly means of producing energy. One such method is using wind power. A new wind power plant in Pushkin Pass, a mountainous area in northern Armenia, has been opened with financial help from the Iranian government. The capacity of the new wind plant is still fairly modest, but this will change over time. Solar energy, although still on a small scale, is also being utilized in Armenian homes today.

GOVERNMENT INITIATIVES TO PROTECT THE ENVIRONMENT

Before Armenia's independence in 1991, there were insufficient laws to protect the environment. Since independence, however, the Armenian government has introduced a series of laws aimed at protecting the ecosystem. These include laws relating to protected areas, a land code, a forest statute, and laws relating to the protection of the country's flora and fauna.

Armenia also developed a biodiversity strategy and action plan aimed at introducing solutions to combat any commercial activity such as logging that may damage the environment. Key objectives of the strategy include

- conserving and restoring forestland and increasing forest area by 7,413 acres (3,000 ha).
- increasing public awareness of biodiversity through education and training.
- allowing nongovernment organizations (NGOs) to participate in projects and take a role in conservation management.
- conserving and regenerating species, ecosystems, and landscapes.

A view of part of Armenia's thick woods in Agartsin.

ARMENIANS

THE ARMENIAN RACE IS ONE OF THE OLDEST races in history. Armenians are the contemporaries of Babylonians, Hittites, Assyrians, and a host of other ancient races.

Armenians call themselves *Hai* and claim descent from Haik, the great-grandson of Japeth, son of Noah. Haik challenged the authority of Babylonian despot Belus, killed him in combat, and gathering his family, settled on what was to become known as the home of the Armenians. This was the beginning of the Armenian state (c. 1200 B.C.).

History shows that the Armenian advance from Cappadocia to the plateau of Erzerum near Mount Ararat (in present-day eastern Turkey) took place between the seventh and eighth centuries B.C. The tribes living in these districts either were absorbed by the Armenians or fled to the north of the Caucasus.

Armenians are considered the most dynamic of the peoples of the former Soviet Union. A long history of repeated invasions has created a tough people with great endurance. Today Armenians experience an outstanding economic growth rate and standards in education and medical science nearing parity with those of Western Europe.

Left: **An Armenian family spending their Sunday together visiting the 13th century Astvatsatsin Church.**

Opposite: **This happy grandfather has likely lived through three Armenias—Turkish Armenia, Soviet Armenia, and now independent Armenia.**

61

A SOCIABLE PEOPLE

Armenia's population stands at nearly 3 million. Almost 70 percent of the population live in urban areas. About 51 percent of the population are female. Age-wise, Armenia's population is in good shape, with the bulk of it (68.4 percent) in the 15-64 age range.

The people of Armenia are the product of ethnic mingling that has been going on for thousands of years in Transcaucasia, due mainly to the many foreign invasions in that area.

As a people, Armenians are extremely sociable, hospitable, and loyal to their family and community. They are deeply attached to their national church, and most of them have a pronounced religious bent. Although often perceived as serious and subdued, Armenians are not devoid of humor. It has been said that their distinguishing characteristic is grit, to which they owe their continued existence as a people.

Growing up in independent Armenia, these sisters will probably live a more westernized adult life than their parents.

ARMENIANS ABROAD

Armenia's long and peppered history of invasions has unsurprisingly resulted in the exodus of Armenians from the country to avoid persecution or simply to escape conquest. Armenian colonies are found in virtually every corner of the globe, from the Americas to Europe to Asia.

Today Armenians in the former Soviet Union, Western Europe, and the United States have risen to the top of all the arts and scientific professions. Armenians are found in key positions in medicine and physics, in teaching and research, and in literature and music.

VICTOR HAMBARTSUMYAN

Armenia has produced its share of prominent personalities in the arts, sports, and academia. Victor Hambartsumyan (1908–96) was one such person.

Born in Tbilisi, Georgia, Hambartsumyan was a prominent astrophysicist who challenged conventional thinking. He suggested that many of the processes involved in the creation and evolution of the universe and of individual galaxies occur during the dispersion and decrease in the density of matter. He demonstrated that galaxies are surrounded by clusters of distinct star types that are unstable and so young that they must still be forming in areas of expansion and density. Hambartsumyan also challenged conventional theories when he disputed the idea that certain stars were formed as a product of galactic collision. He believed that they were produced through colossal explosions in the nuclei of normal galaxies.

The son of an eminent Armenian philologist, Victor Hambartsumyan inherited his father's brilliant academic mind. He majored in mathematics and physics and graduated from the Leningrad State University in 1928 before going to the Pulkovo Observatory to earn his doctorate, which he received in 1931. Hambartsumyan was appointed to a lectureship at Leningrad and after just three years was made a professor. But the political climate in Russia at that time was unfavorable, and Hambartsumyan and his team found themselves in conflict with the director of the Pulkovo Observatory. After much dispute, the observatory was destroyed.

By the 1940s the Soviet government had decided to invest in science as a tool to shore up Communist ideologies, and a new era of research began. Hambartsumyan was appointed head of astrophysics at Yerevan University in Armenia. Here he saw to the construction of the Byurakan Observatory, which sits 13,000 feet (3,962 m) high on Mount Aragats.

Hambartsumyan was a man of strong convictions and beliefs. In 1989 he went on a three-week hunger strike in an attempt to draw public and government attention to the conflict in Nagorno-Karabakh. He was twice awarded the Soviet Union's highest honor, the Hero of Socialist Labor medal. After the collapse of the Soviet Union, he was also awarded the National Hero of Armenia medal.

Victor Hambartsumyan was a world-renowned astrophysicist; William Saroyan achieved international fame as a novelist and storyteller; Aram Khachaturian was a household name in operatic and orchestral music; and Charles Aznavour is a popular figure in light music and song. The London musical scene was enriched by Armenian violinist Manoug Parikian and critic Felix Aprahamian, while in Europe and America operatic stages have been graced by Lynne Dourian and Luisa Bosabalian. Singapore's world-famous Raffles Hotel, which provided accommodations to such distinguished guests as Somerset Maugham, was built and originally owned by well known Armenian entrepreneurs the Sarkies brothers.

ARMENIANS IN ISTANBUL

Prior to 1453, the year Fatih Sultan Mehmet conquered Constantinople (now Istanbul, in Turkey), few Armenians resided in the Byzantine capital. In fact, after Mehmet's conquest, many of those few Armenian inhabitants fled the city. The population of the city then was 40,000, the majority of whom were Greeks. To augment the population,

Mehmet ordered his administrators to bring people from all areas of Anatolia. Many were brought by force, and many of these were Armenians.

Although there were people of many races and faiths living in the Ottoman Empire—Armenians, Turks, and other Asians, who were Muslims, Christians, or Jews—the Armenian community was considered the most loyal to the empire. The Turkish authorities called the Armenian community *millet-i sadika* (MIL-ay-ee SAH-dee-KAH), which in Turkish means "the loyal nation." Their loyalty saw many Armenians serving the Ottoman government and army.

The exact population of Armenians in Istanbul today is not known, as many do not register themselves.

Above: **Armenian-American writer William Saroyan was awarded the Pulitzer Prize in 1940 for his play** *The Time of Your Life.*

THE MINORITIES

The minority races in Armenia enjoy equal rights and freedom to practice their religions and cultures, rights that are clearly defined in the country's

Opposite: **Armenian-born French singer Charles Aznavour smiles for the camera upon arrival at the 58th Cannes Film Festival in May 2005.**

ARMENIANS IN THE UNITED STATES

The exact number of Armenians living in the United States is not known, although unofficial estimates are from 500,000 to 2 million. The Armenian community has integrated well into the country, even playing an active role in politics. A number of Armenians have become successful entrepreneurs. One famous American of Armenian origin is tennis star Andre Agassi.

The Jewish community in Armenia has its own cultural center and a Sunday school. The school has about 200 students, half of whom are adults.

declaration of independence. The government has adopted policies encouraging the minority communities to develop their own cultures and educate their communities.

Russians make up a significant part of the minority population in Armenia. Apart from them, there are Kurds and Yezidis, who live mainly in the rural areas. Though the language spoken by Yezidis is Kurdish, they tend to regard themselves as distinct from the Kurds.

The Kurdish community in Armenia is very active. There is a Kurdological Department of the Institute of Oriental Studies at the Yerevan State University and a Kurdish Writers Union of Armenia. In addition, Yerevan has been a center of Kurdish publishing activity for some decades, as well as the center for Kurdish broadcasting, not only to Kurds in Armenia and the rest of Transcaucasia but also to Kurds abroad, primarily in Turkey and Iran.

After the end of seven decades of Soviet rule, many Armenian Jews are coming forward to assert their Jewish identity. The Jewish community in Armenia dates back to the first century A.D., when Tigran the Great resettled 10,000 Jews in Armenia following his retreat from Palestine. The most recent wave of Jews arrived during World War II, as Armenia offered a safe haven for those driven away from the Nazi-occupied areas of Russia, Belarus, and Ukraine.

KURDS

Kurd is the ethnic name of a number of tribal groups inhabiting the mountainous border regions of southeastern Turkey, northwestern Iran, northern Iraq, northeastern Syria, rural Armenia, and Azerbaijan generally known as Kurdistan. The Kurds, most of whom are Sunni Muslims, speak various dialects of Kurdish, an Indo-Iranian language.

The Kurds resemble their neighbors in southwestern Asia, although they tend to have a fairer complexion. Their population is estimated at 35 million, about 55 percent of whom live in Turkey, about 20 percent each in Iran and Iraq, and a bit more than 5 percent in Syria.

Most Kurds live in rural villages, cultivating wheat, barley, cotton, and fruit. Some are nomads, but their numbers have dwindled since the closing of national frontiers and the Kurdish political struggles of the past several decades. The traditional Kurdish tribal system is based on descent, with the leaders having immense power.

Although the Kurds have never been united politically, Kurdish autonomy has had a long history. *Kurd* as a collective name was first applied to the tribal groups in the seventh century A.D. when they converted to Islam. Three short-lived Kurdish dynasties existed in the 10th–12th centuries. The 12th-century Kurdish warrior Saladin, a prominent foe of the Crusaders, founded another dynasty that lasted into the 13th century. During succeeding centuries numerous Kurdish principalities vied for local power, showing little interest in achieving unity. Only in the late 19th and early 20th centuries did a nationalist movement emerge. With the breakup of the Ottoman Empire after World War I, Turkey agreed to the establishment of an independent Kurdistan under the Treaty of Sevres in 1920. This part of the treaty was never ratified, however, and the autonomy clause was completely eliminated from the 1923 Treaty of Lausanne through Turkish efforts under Mustafa Kemal Ataturk, the first president of the Republic of Turkey.

Kurds in Iran launched an unsuccessful uprising after the 1979 Islamic revolution, and Kurdish separatist guerrillas remain active in Turkey despite Turkish efforts to assimilate the nation's Kurdish population. Most nationalist activity since 1946 has been in Iraq, however. The Kurds waged guerrilla warfare against the Iraqi government in 1961–70 and open rebellion in 1974–75. This movement collapsed when unofficial Iranian support was withdrawn after a 1975 Iran-Iraq border accord. Iraqi Kurdish separatists later backed Iran in the Iran-Iraq war of 1980–88. In 1988 the Iraqi government was accused of using chemical weapons against the Kurds. Iraqi Kurds again revolted after Iraq's defeat in the 1991 Persian Gulf War. When the rebellion failed, more than a million Iraqi Kurds fled their homes. As the death toll among the Kurds mounted, U.S. military forces built camps for them in northern Iraq. The administration of these camps was later assumed by the United Nations. In April 1992 Iraqi Kurds held their first elections free of Iraqi control to choose a leader and a Kurdish National Assembly. More than 100,000 Iraqi Kurds are thought to have been killed since the mid-1970s, however, and the Kurdish zone in northern Iraq remains under an Iraqi economic blockade. The Kurds there fear further attacks by Iraqi military forces.

LIFESTYLE

ARMENIA PLACES A HIGH PRIORITY on educating its population. According to official statistics, 99 percent of Armenia's population is literate. Armenia has a well-developed system of higher educational institutions and scientific research and technological institutes. This network has been instrumental in supporting the development of several high-tech industries in Armenia.

The National Plan for Education Development 2001–05 was approved by the parliament in June 2001. The plan stresses the development of an educated population. The government believes this is the key to achieving a progressive and socio-economically developed nation. The government's emphasis on educating the population has produced results—31 percent of eligible children are enrolled in preprimary school, 94 percent are

Left: **Armenian women living in the countryside fetching water from a pipe by a railway station.**

Opposite: **A caretaker of a church in Echmiadzin hoeing weeds.**

enrolled in primary school, 84 percent are in secondary school, and 26 percent have graduated from one of the many universities in the country. Many Armenians also go abroad for postgraduate education.

EDUCATION

Education, which has always played a central role in Armenia, is compulsory and free at elementary and high school levels. Children must have at least eight years of schooling between the ages of six and 16. After that they have an option to go to college or vocational school.

The language in institutions of higher learning is Armenian, although Russian is also taught. There are 25 public institutions of higher education (including seven colleges) and 40 private educational institutions.

The leading educational institutions, such as the Yerevan State University, the Yerevan State Medical University, the Yerevan State Institute for Russian and Foreign Languages, and the Yerevan Komitas Conservatory, are recognized for outstanding achievements in their fields.

Armenia's high educational standards have given rise to many inventions by Armenian scientists and engineers. Armenian researchers have developed many internationally marketable technologies. One successful product developed in the Armenian Academy of Science is a baby food called Narine, which has therapeutic and nutritive qualities and was licensed to the Japanese Miki Trading Company.

HUMAN RIGHTS

The Armenian government has adopted international conventions on human, civil, and political rights, as well as universal standards of freedom of conscience and religion. This is clearly stated in the second chapter of Armenia's constitution.

The state respects citizens' constitutional right to freedom of association, as can be seen by the existence of more than 60 political parties and thousands of nongovernment organizations (NGOs). However, civil servants and other public sector employees are forced to campaign for existing office bearers and ruling parties during elections.

The Armenian media operate in a somewhat hostile environment. The state-owned Armenian Public Television and almost all private channels are tightly controlled.

The creation in 2003 of Armenia's Office of the Human Rights Defender gave citizens an important avenue for seeking justice. Although the organization's first head, Larisa Alaverdian, was appointed by the president, it has proven to be quite vocal in condemning and tackling abuses committed by various government bodies. However, Alaverdian was forced to resign on account of political pressure.

A class outing to a memorial statue commemorating Armenia's independence. Having been subjugated and persecuted for much of their long history, Armenians included human-rights guarantees in their constitution.

The constitution gives equal rights and protection to ethnic minorities (mostly Yezidis, Kurds, Russians, and Assyrians), who make up less than 3 percent of the country's population.

HEALTH AND SOCIAL WELFARE

A considerable portion of Armenia's health and social welfare system is still predominantly financed by the state budget. Much of Armenia's expenditure on health and welfare services has been directed toward

A hospital in Armenia. Armenia's health-care system is supplemented by medical aid from humanitarian organizations.

the victims of the 1988 earthquake, which killed an estimated 25,000 people and caused $5 billion worth of damage. Armenia's conflict with Azerbaijan over the territory of Nagorno-Karabakh, coupled with the collapse of the Soviet Union, also saw the migration of a large number of refugees into Armenia, creating new demands on social expenditure and putting more pressure on the national budget.

Although the state has been allocating more money to health care (from 18 percent of the total budget in 2004 to 24 percent in 2005), it is still not enough to meet the needs of Armenians. The government is responsible for providing health services for the entire population. In reality, however, only certain groups (such as the disabled) have coverage.

In 1998, with the World Bank's assistance, the Armenian government introduced the Basic Benefits Package (BBP). This package lists medical services that are covered by the government and specifies the population groups that are entitled to the services.

Privatization in the health sector has been slower than in other sectors of the economy. Almost all pharmacies and medical technical services have been privatized, but only a third of dental clinics have moved in this direction.

ARMENIAN REFUGEES

Armenia's continuing conflict with Azerbaijan has created a community of refugees in Armenia. In 1988 Nagorno-Karabakh, a predominantly ethnic Armenian enclave within Azerbaijan, voted to secede and join Armenia. Armenian support for the separatists led to an economic blockade by Azerbaijan (joined by Turkey), which crippled Armenia's foreign trade and restricted imports of food and fuel. This blockade is still in place today.

Ethnic Azeris who fled or were deported from Armenia in 1988 and 1989 remain refugees, primarily in Azerbaijan. Armenia, in turn, has received the lion's share of the roughly 400,000 ethnic Armenians who have fled Azerbaijan since 1988. Many of these refugees are still living in temporary houses and refugee camps. Providing for them has put an enormous burden on Armenia's already overtaxed welfare budget.

Thousands of Armenian refugees are housed in temporary shelters.

In Armenia's busy cities, many grandmothers double as day-care providers for their grandchildren and help to babysit and nurture them while their daughters are at work.

WOMEN IN ARMENIA

Women in Armenia have come a long way since the country declared independence. While women living in the rural areas may still be somewhat traditional and play roles limited to looking after families and bearing children, urban women have started to enter the labor market. Part of the reason is that the cost of living in the cities is higher, necessitating a two-income family.

The lot of urban working women in Armenia is similar to that of working women in other countries. Although many work full-time to help augment the family income, the main burden of housework and child care still rests firmly on their shoulders.

The advent of women into the labor market and the attendant issues of child care, unequal pay between the genders, and the glass ceiling have resulted in the creation of many women's groups. One of the best

known and successful is Shamiram, a political party that now has eight members as deputies in the National Assembly. In spite of their double burden of career and household duties, many Armenian women, such as opera singer Gohar Gasparian and pianist Svetlana Navasardian, have made an impact in the international arena.

NATIONAL DRESS

The Armenian national dress has several variations, depending on what area of Armenia the wearer is from. Generally Armenian women wear long skirts with an apron under an ornately trimmed blouse or caftan. Some women wear wide trousers. The women also wear elaborate jewelry and headgear. Their shoes or boots have toes pointing upward.

Men generally wear wide trousers, a long-sleeve waistcoat, and some kind of turban. The men's boots also turn up at the toe end.

The traditional dress of Yezidi women from the area around Gyumri in the northwest consists of a red velvet unlined garment with a velvet apron lined with printed calico. The hem of the dress and the edges of

Members of a women's choir with headscarves.

the apron are usually trimmed with a zigzag design. An ornate quilted garment made of pieces of colored silk adorned with glass beads and buttons is tied to the chest with strings around the neck and the waist. High soft leather boots decorated with appliqué and impressed designs are worn over ankle-high leather shoes.

SHAMIRAM

Shamiram, or the Armenian Women's Union, was founded in April 1995 to champion and safeguard women's rights and increase the involvement of women in the fields of policy, decision-making, and democratic and market reforms. The party's aim is to improve and expand social programs, medical care, and education for all Armenians. The group is also strongly against the current tax policy, which is considered an overwhelming burden for the average Armenian household.

Eight out of the 12 women deputies in the National Assembly are Shamiram members: Zaruhi Arevshatian, Anzhela Bakunts, Juliet Kazhoyan, Shogher Matevosian, Amalya Petrosian, Nadezhda Sargisian, Gayane Sarukhanian, and Anahit Torosian.

Shogher Matevosian heads Shamiram, and the party is estimated to have a membership of about 4,400 women.

Women from northwestern Armenia wear caftans made of coarse striped silk decorated with thin gold braid around the neckline. The front of the caftan is edged with silk-covered buttons. The long sleeves are further lengthened with false sleeves in a contrasting color to imitate an undergarment. The false sleeves are also cut in a zigzag pattern and decorated with gold braid. The caps that these women wear have long silk tassels.

Women from this region also wear short silk damask jackets edged with gold cord over wide trousers. The sleeves of the jacket end in a point. The trousers are generally made of a coarser silk than the jacket. The leather slippers that they wear, with the toes pointing upward, are embroidered in red.

Part of the traditional dress of a male Kurd from the Yerevan area is wide trousers elaborately trimmed with silk and gold cord. These are fastened around the waist with a drawstring. The sleeved waistcoats that they wear are styled after the caftan and are almost always of a striped fabric, closing with small buttons at the neck. Gold braid is sometimes added down the front to give the impression of an ornate fastening.

A woman in 16th-century Armenian dress. Traditional Armenian clothes have changed relatively little over the centuries.

RELIGION

CHRISTIANITY IS THE dominant religion in Armenia. Most Armenian Christians belong to the Armenian Apostolic Church, but there is also a sizable Russian Orthodox minority. The other large minority religion is Islam, although the number of Muslims in the country has dwindled due to the departure of most Azeris.

Prior to the adoption of Christianity as the state religion in A.D. 301, Armenian beliefs were reflected by the religions prevalent in the Mediterranean and Eastern Europe.

Above: **Although Armenia was the first state to adopt Christianity as a national religion, some older customs have persisted. For example, in ancient times, Armenians considered trees to be sacred plants with the power to grant special requests. By tying strips of cloth to a tree, one could ask for help or heal sick relatives and friends. Some Armenians continue this practice today.**

Opposite: **Carved cross at Echmiadzin Cathedral, built in 480 and located in a walled compound in Ararat where Jesus is believed to have descended from heaven to show where a church should be built.**

During the fifth century B.C., while under the rule of the Persian Empire, Armenians adopted the Persian gods. Ahura-Mazda, father of the gods, was worshiped as Aramazd, while Mithra, god of light and justice, was known as Mihr. Anahita, goddess of fertility and mother of all wisdom, became Anahit, the favorite goddess of the Armenians.

Under Alexander the Great, Armenia entered the Hellenistic orbit and, like most other peoples in the ancient world, were able to harmonize their pantheon with the Greek one. Early Greek priests brought statues of their gods to Armenia and placed them in Hellenistic temples. As a result, a Persian-Greco religion as well as the worship of local deities existed until the adoption of Christianity in the fourth century.

The Armenian Apostolic Church, established by the apostles Thaddeus and Bartholomew, preserves its national exclusiveness, recognizes the supremacy of no other spiritual jurisdiction, and considers itself the equal of the Roman Catholic and Greek Orthodox churches.

Echmiadzin Cathedral is the spiritual center of the Armenian Church and the seat of the Catholicos of All Armenians. It is also the oldest cathedral and Christian monastery in the world.

While the majority of the population of Armenia (about 94 percent) belong to the Armenian Apostolic Church, there is also a small community belonging to the Russian Orthodox Church. Apart from that, there are Yezidis who practice Zoroastrianism, followers of other types of Christianity, Muslims, and a small community of Jews.

THE ARMENIAN APOSTOLIC CHURCH

The Armenian Church is one of the oldest churches in Christendom. The gospel was preached in Armenia by the apostles Thaddeus and Bartholomew in the first century, establishing the apostolic origins of their church.

Armenian martyrologies carry the names of many Christian bishops dating back to the first century. The names of some of these martyrs are included in the ecclesiastical history of Eusebius of Caesarea (c. A.D. 260–340), who is regarded as the first historian of Christianity.

When the Council of Nicaea was held in A.D. 325 to establish a common creed, 318 bishops attended, each representing an independent church of equal status. Armenia was represented by Aristakes, a son and successor of Gregory the Illuminator. The Armenian Church, although jurisdictionally independent from the others beginning in the fourth century, separated from the Greek and Latin churches in the middle of the sixth century regarding a difference of opinion on the Council of Chalcedon (A.D. 451). The Armenian Church, like the West Syriac Orthodox, Coptic, and Ethiopian churches, does not accept the Council of Chalcedon and its definition of the relationship between the humanity and the divinity in Christ. This schism led to great conflict with the Byzantine Church, which frequently resorted to persecution and mass deportations in attempts to bring the Armenians in line with its beliefs.

Later, during the period of the Cilician kingdom of the Armenians and at the time of the Crusades, this independence brought the Armenians into contention with the Roman Catholic Church. In more modern times, it separated Armenians from the Russian Orthodox Church and the Czarist government.

As a national institution, the Armenian Apostolic Church has played an important role in Armenian history, at times assuming both political and spiritual leadership. The church adopts this dual role even today.

The fall of the ruling dynasty during the fifth century may have ended the Armenian kingdom, but the head of the church became the enduring symbol of national unity and the rallying point of patriotism. Through the centuries, Armenians at home and abroad have regarded the Catholicos of Echmiadzin not only as the head of their church but also as their spokesperson and elected representative.

CHURCH RITUALS AND HIERARCHY

The Armenian Church places great importance on the liturgy, which has remained virtually unchanged since the 10th century. The liturgical music with characteristically Armenian notations dates back to the 11th century. The liturgy is in classical Armenian, and the homily is in modern Armenian.

The Armenian Church has been the Armenian people's unifying force throughout centuries of foreign invasions, occupation, and forced migration. Christianity remains strong in Armenia despite the many efforts to stifle it during the Soviet period. The Armenian Church combined nationalism and religion as its policy for safeguarding Armenian culture.

The patriarch of the Armenian Cathedral in Jerusalem. Liturgy and ritual are very important aspects of the Armenian Church.

The Holy Orders of the Armenian Church are the diaconate, the priesthood, and the episcopate. Deacons and parish priests may marry, but they must do so before they are ordained. All other orders are celibate, including *vardapets* (VAHR-dah-pets), who are monastic priests. Bishops are chosen from this rank. The episcopate, the highest rank, consists of bishops and archbishops, the patriarchs of Constantinople (Istanbul) and Jerusalem, the Catholicos of Cilicia, and the Supreme Patriarch and Catholicos of All Armenians.

The Supreme Patriarch's seat is the Holy See of Echmiadzin, near Yerevan. His authority is universal throughout Armenia and the diaspora. For historical reasons, however, since the 15th century the Catholicos of Cilicia has maintained separate jurisdictions, which now include Armenian churches in Syria, Lebanon, Iran, and Greece and two prelacies in the United States. The Supreme Patriarch exercises authority and leadership through the two patriarchs and through prelates (archbishops and bishops) elected locally and confirmed by him in their diocese.

CATHOLICOS OF ALL ARMENIANS

"Catholicos of All Armenians" is the highest title to be bestowed in the Armenian Church. The Catholicos is elected by the National Religious Assembly.

The current Catholicos of All Armenians is Archbishop Karekin II, born Ktrich Nersessian. He succeeded Karekin I, born Neshan Sarkissian, who died in June 1999.

Karekin II was born in 1951 in the village of Voskehat, near Echmiadzin. He graduated from the Seminary of Holy Echmiadzin in 1971 with honors and was ordained a deacon in 1970 and a monk in 1972.

In June 1983 he was designated head of Araratian Pontifical Diocese and in October of the same year was appointed bishop by His Holiness Vasken I. He rose to the title of archbishop in November 1992. With the death of Catholicos Vasken I, Archbishop Nersessian became a candidate for the pontifical throne but conceded victory to His Holiness Sarkissian. Catholicos Karekin I succumbed to cancer in June 1999, and the Armenian Church elected Nersessian his successor in October of the same year.

In his role, Catholicos Karekin II rules over the Supreme Spiritual Council, which is the Armenian Church's governing college of bishops, and is the chief shepherd of the world's 7 million Armenian Apostolic Christians.

THE RUSSIAN ORTHODOX CHURCH

Members of the Russian Orthodox Church make up the largest religious minority in Armenia. The church, which marked its 1,000th anniversary in 1988, is the largest and most influential of all Orthodox churches.

The origin of the Russian Church dates back to the "baptism of Russia" in A.D. 988. The Russian Church was originally headed by Byzantine metropolitans appointed by the patriarch of Constantinople.

In 1448 the independence of the Russian Church was proclaimed. It was then headed by metropolitans elected by a council of Russian hierarchs, who did not have to be approved by the patriarch of Constantinople.

The title of patriarch was abolished in 1721 when Czar Peter the Great failed to get the patriarch's support for his reforms. Peter replaced the

Orthodoxy is a term of self-definition by which adherents of one set of theological, dogmatic, and political beliefs contrast themselves with those of a different set whom they label heterodox. The original Christian Church was founded by the apostles in the first century A.D. Ultimately, five great sees were given the designation of patriarchate. These were Rome, Constantinople, Alexandria, Antioch, and Jerusalem. Rome was designated first, in recognition that this was the seat of secular power at the outset of Christianity; Constantinople was designated next when this became the seat of the Holy Roman Empire, Emperor Constantine having decided in A.D. 324 to shift his capital from Rome to Byzantium; Alexandria and Antioch were designated as they were seats of great learning; and Jerusalem, although much smaller in extent and influence, was included as a special mark of respect for the Holy Land.

Bishops attended and participated as equals in periodic councils—the Council of Nicaea (A.D. 325) and the Council of Chalcedon (A.D. 451) are two examples. Major decisions, including those on dogma, doctrine, and heresies, were made at these councils.

The first major division between different Christian traditions occurred in the aftermath of the Council of Chalcedon, which was not accepted by all Christians.

Four Orthodox priests in front of their church. The Russian Orthodox Church is the largest minority religion in Armenia.

patriarch with the Holy Governing Synod, whose members were appointed by the czar, and the synod administered the Russian Church. This system was abolished in 1917 when the Local Council of 1917–18 restored the patriarchate.

ISLAM

The Muslim community in Armenia makes up 1-2 percent of the population. Islam is practiced by the Kurdish community and, to a lesser extent, by the Yezidis.

Islam in Arabic means "to surrender," but as a religious term in the Koran it means "to surrender to the will or law of God." It was through Prophet Muhammad—who began to preach a series of revelations granted to him by Allah (Arabic for "God")—that Islam was introduced. The two fundamental sources of Islamic doctrine and practice are the Koran and the Sunnah.

Muslims regard the Koran as the word of God as told to Muhammad through Gabriel, the angel of revelation. They believe that God himself, not Muhammad, is the author and therefore that the Koran is infallible. The Koran is the collection of the passages revealed to Muhammad during the approximately 22 years of his prophetic life (610–32).

The second substantive source of Islam, the Sunnah, or "example of the Prophet," is known through Hadith, the body of traditions based on what the Prophet said or did regarding various issues. Unlike the Koran, which was memorized by early Muslims and compiled in written form quite early, the transmission of Hadith was largely verbal, and the present authoritative collections date from the ninth century.

The tiled dome of Gok Jami mosque in Yerevan.

Unlike the Koran, Hadith is not considered infallible. During the early days of Islam, whether the Prophet himself was infallible (apart from the revelations in the Koran) was a point of controversy. Later, however, the consensus of the Islamic community was that both he and the earlier prophets were infallible. Because Hadith was mainly transmitted orally, however, it was conceded that error could enter into the human transmission. Hadith, therefore, is a source secondary to the Koran.

JUDAISM

Few in number, the Jews represent the smallest minority group in Armenia. Judaism originated in Israel. A rich and complex religious tradition, Judaism has certain characteristics. The most essential of these is a radical monotheism—that is, the belief that a single, transcendent God created and still continues to govern the universe. Supporting this monotheism is the belief that the world is both intelligible and purposive, because a single divine intelligence stands behind it. Therefore, nothing that humanity experiences is capricious; everything ultimately has meaning.

To the traditional Jew, the mind of God is manifested both in the natural order, through creation, and in the socio-historical order, through revelation. Jews believe that the same God who created the world revealed himself to the Israelites at Mount Sinai. This revelation is contained in the Torah (which means "revealed instruction" in Hebrew); God's will for humankind is expressed in commandments by which individuals are to regulate their lives in their interactions with one another and with God. Only by living in accordance with God's laws and submitting to the divine will can humanity become a harmonious part of the cosmos.

A second major concept in Judaism is that of the covenant (*berith*), or "contractual agreement," between God and the Jewish people. According

Both biblical authors and later Jewish traditionalists view the covenant between God and the Jews in a universal context. To them, only after successive failures to establish a covenant with rebellious humanity did God turn to a particular segment of it. Israel is to be a "kingdom of priests," and the ideal social order it establishes in accordance with the divine laws is to be a model for the human race. Israel thus stands between God and humanity, representing each to the other.

to tradition, the God of creation entered into a special relationship with the Jews at Sinai. The Jews would acknowledge God as their sole, ultimate king and legislator, agreeing to obey his laws; God, in turn, would acknowledge Israelites as his chosen people and be especially mindful of them.

ZOROASTRIANISM

Zoroastrians believe in one god, Ahura-Mazda. Zoroastrianism thrived under various Persian dynasties, and at one point the Persian Empire spanned the entire "civilized" world—from eastern Greece to northern India. Remnants of the religion were left in Europe, including the cult of Mithraism, which was spread by the Roman army.

Alexander's defeat of the Persian Alchaemenid dynasty did not destroy Zoroastrianism. The religion continued under the Parthians and then flourished under the Sasanians. It was only with the Islamic conquest of Persia that Zoroastrianism began to decline, though this was a lengthy process. Many of the wealthiest families in India are still Parsis—Zoroastrians of Persian descent.

All Zoroastrians must wear the *sudra-kusti* (SOOD-rah KOOS-ti). The *sudra* is a white cotton tunic, and the *kusti* is a woolen string worn around the waist on top of the *sudra*. The tying of the *kusti* is a part of the basic daily prayers of a Zoroastrian.

The Zoroastrians have a very high regard for the Creation and in particular for the elements fire and water.

Prayers are recited only in the sacred language, Avestan. The Zoroastrian book of daily prayers is called the Khordeh Avesta (Selected Avesta). It is a collection of prayers selected from other major Avestan works such as Yasna, the Vispurad, the Vendidad, and the Yasht.

Zoroastrianism was founded in ancient Persia by the prophet Zarathushtra and is considered to be the world's first monotheistic religion.

ՈՒԹՈՅԱՆ ԴՈՐԿԱ

ՅԱՆ ԳԵԴԵՈՆ

ՅԱՆ ԱՀՐՈՒԻԿ

ԿԱՆ ԿՈՆՍՏԱՆՏ

ՅԻՆ ՍԱՐԳԻ

LANGUAGE

THE OFFICIAL ADOPTION of Christianity by King Tiridates III in A.D. 301 started a new phase in the spiritual and intellectual life of the Armenian people. The advent of Christianity meant that the founders of the Armenian Church had to set themselves the task of translating the Bible and the essential liturgical books into Armenian. The first line to be translated into Armenian was Proverbs 1:1.

Both Greek and Syriac Christianity had a profound influence on the early development of Christianity in Armenia. Scriptural readings and the liturgy had previously been chanted in Greek or Syriac (a form of Aramaic). There is some evidence that these were simultaneously translated into Armenian for the congregants. A major obstacle to the task of translating was that the Armenian language was primarily an oral language and had, as yet, no alphabet of its own. The difficult but vital task of inventing the alphabet for the Armenian language was ultimately achieved in A.D. 406 by an Armenian monk, Mesrop Mashtots.

With the alphabet evolved the classical Armenian language known as Grabar, or "book language." The first work of literature with the new alphabet was the translation of the Bible from Greek. Thereafter, numerous literary works, both originals and translations, were written in Grabar.

Although Grabar prevailed for a long time in literature and church texts, it gradually lagged behind as Armenia pursued a national language. Subsequently Grabar fell into disuse because it was incomprehensible to the masses. Toward the end of the 19th century, Ashkharabar, a new literary language understandable across dialects, was formed and eventually became the country's national language.

Above: **Manuscripts from Yerevan's Matenadaran Institute. The institute has approximately 25,000 manuscripts, including treatises on history, philosophy, law, medicine, mathematics, and geography, as well as works of literature and miniature paintings.**

Opposite: **Old Armenian script carved on stone.**

THE ARMENIAN ALPHABET

The lack of an alphabet made it impossible for Armenians to have a literature of their own. As the state was challenged by foreign foes, it was necessary for the Armenians to have their own literature if they were to survive as a people. With the encouragement of Catholicos Sahag and King Vramshabouh, Mesrop Mashtots devised an alphabet that had 36 letters. (Three were added later.)

The Armenian alphabet was devised to represent Armenian sounds. It is believed to have been influenced by Syriac, Pahlavi (a Persian language), and to a lesser extent, Greek.

The original alphabet was written in large capital letters. Between the 10th and 11th centuries, a type of curved initials called *boloragits yerkatagir* (boh-loh-RAH-gitz yuhr-KAH-tah-GEER), or "iron capitals," was used. The "middle" *yerkatagir* of the 11th and 12th centuries had more straight lines, and there is also a lower-case *yerkatagir* script. Sometimes a combination of more than one style of *yerkatagir* occurs, referred to as "mixed letters." Since the 13th century, the predominant script has been the small *bologir* (boh-loh-GEER) writing. In the 18th century, a form of cursive writing was developed.

The invention of an Armenian alphabet allowed the translation of all the major works of the classical age and the writing of original Armenian works. This period was the golden age of Armenian literature and occurred just before Armenia was divided by Rome and Persia, which brought an end to the Armenian dynasty. Armenian culture survived through its alphabet and literature.

Toward the end of the 19th century, 246 newspapers and journals in Armenian were being published all over the world. At the beginning of the 20th century the number increased to 724.

Throughout a long history of invasions many Armenians had fled Armenia, setting up communities all over the world. These Armenians had to be enterprising to survive in a foreign country, thus many became merchants, academics, or artists.

The first Armenian book was printed in Venice, Italy, in 1512. The first map of the world to be printed in Armenian was produced by Armenian cartographers and engravers in Amsterdam, the Netherlands, in 1694; the first Armenian journal was published in Madras, India, in 1794.

EASTERN AND WESTERN ARMENIAN DIALECTS

By the 19th century two major Armenian dialects—Eastern Armenian and Western Armenian—had evolved. Both are still used today. Each dialect has two "r" sounds, three "ch" sounds, three "t" sounds, and two "p" sounds. In Western Armenian, some of the distinctions between the soft "t" and the middle "t" have disappeared; in Eastern Armenian, the sounds are distinct. The other difference lies in the conjugation of verbs. The present tense in Western Armenian looks like the future tense in Eastern Armenian.

Learning a second language.

OTHER LANGUAGES

The official language of the country is Armenian. However, Armenia's long association with the former Soviet Union has meant that many people in Armenia are well versed in written and spoken Russian.

Part of the Indo-European family of Slavic languages, Russian uses the Cyrillic alphabet, which is made up of 33 letters. Spelling is basically, though not completely, phonetic, and the rules of pronunciation are few and simple.

The Russian language has no articles, either definite or indefinite. All Russian nouns fall into one of three grammatical genders: the masculine, the feminine, and the neuter.

MESROP MASHTOTS

Mesrop Mashtots (361–440), the creator of the Armenian alphabet, was born in the province of Taron. He graduated from one of the schools established by Catholicos Nerses the Great. A man of exceptional ability who had mastered Greek, Syriac, Persian, and other languages, Mashtots was soon appointed as royal secretary in the city of Vagharshapat, or Echmiadzin, then the capital of Armenia. After a few years of government service, Mashtots resigned from his post and entered the Armenian Church.

Around the age of 40, Mashtots began preaching in different parts of Armenia. It was in the course of these tours that he conceived the idea of inventing an Armenian alphabet with the objective of translating the Bible. He realized that this would both help propagate the Christian faith and establish a strong tie to bind together Armenians living in eastern and western Armenia and elsewhere. Mashtots and his pupils set to work and completed the task in A.D. 405.

The original set of characters in the alphabet that Mashtots and his disciples devised is still in use today, though written in modern, cursive script. This is a great tribute to the remarkable pioneer, who passed away at a ripe old age of 79.

Mashtots is buried in the crypt of the church at Oshakan, not far from Echmiadzin. The shrine is guarded to this day by a lineal descendant of Mashtots's patron and protector, Vahan Amatuni.

Adjectives agree with nouns in gender, case, and number. The verb has three tenses, present, past, and future; in addition it has the category of aspect. The two aspects are the imperfective, presenting the action as a process of repetition, and the perfective, presenting the action as a unified whole.

A typical feature of Russian vocabulary is large families of words derived from the same root by means of adding various prefixes and suffixes.

In addition to Armenian and Russian, some major Western languages, such as Spanish, Italian, German, French, and especially English, are included in the public school curriculum and are taught in most colleges and universities.

"THE WISE WEAVER"—AN ARMENIAN FOLKTALE

One upon a time, the king was seated on his throne when an ambassador arrived from a distant land. Without saying a word, the ambassador drew a circle around the throne, then sat down and remained silent. The king was puzzled. He summoned all his counselors and asked them what the envoy meant. But none of them could give him an answer.

The king was upset and offended. Was there not a single wise man among his courtiers and advisers? He gave his courtiers strict orders to find a man in his kingdom wise enough to know the answer; otherwise he would slay them all.

With the incentive of keeping their heads if they succeeded, the courtiers wasted no time going around the city looking for such a man. In a poor part of the city, they happened to enter a house where they saw a cradle with a baby in it rocking by itself. There was no one else in the house. They saw the same thing in the next house: the cradle rocking by itself and nobody in the building. When they went up to

the roof they saw a stick moving by itself to frighten away the birds from the grain that was washed and spread out to dry in the sun.

The king's courtiers were amazed. They went down one floor below, where they saw a weaver working at his loom. He had a string tied to one end of the shuttle, a string to the other end, and a third string tied to the comb.

As the shuttle moved back and forth over the loom, the two cradles and the stick set on the roof for frightening the birds away moved with it. A clever weaver indeed.

"An ambassador came from another land and drew a circle around the king's throne but refuses to speak," the courtiers said to the weaver. "We do not know what he means. Maybe you know. Come with us. The king will reward you well if you can solve this puzzle."

The weaver thought it over for a moment, then agreed to go with the courtiers to the king's castle. But he said he had to get a few things first. He took a couple of knucklebones and a pullet and put them in his coat. Then he set off to the king's palace with the courtiers.

On reaching the palace, the weaver took out the knucklebones and threw them before the ambassador. The ambassador took a fistful of millet from his pocket and scattered it on the floor. At this, the weaver pulled out his pullet from under his coat and let it eat the grain.

The ambassador then stood up and departed, without saying a word.

The king and the courtiers were all amazed at this series of events. "What does it mean?" they asked the weaver.

"By drawing a circle around the king's throne, the ambassador meant that his king is coming to besiege our city," answered the weaver, "and he wanted to know whether our king would submit or fight. When I threw my knucklebones before him, I meant they should go and play with knucklebones—they are nothing but children to us, and it is foolish of them to pretend they could fight our king. By scattering the millet on the floor, he meant that his king has innumerable warriors at his command. However, when my pullet ate all the millet, the ambassador understood what I meant—that one of us can slaughter a thousand such warriors."

The king was so pleased with the weaver that he wanted to make him the new chamberlain. But the weaver respectfully declined, preferring to go back to his loom.

"But I implore you, O King," the weaver said, "not to forget that among your humblest servants there are men wiser than your counselors, and I hope from now on your courtiers will treat the weaver and the cobbler with respect."

ARTS

ARMENIA'S LONG HISTORY and mix of cultures has had a profound impact on its arts. Although much of Armenia's rich heritage in the arts extant today dates from A.D. 301, when Christianity became the state religion, the arts of pre-Christian Armenia are also significant, especially those from the ninth to sixth centuries B.C., when Armenia was part of the Urartian kingdom.

The Urartians were major producers of bronze objects. Excavations at Karmir Blur, begun in 1939 and continuing today, have uncovered household utensils, furniture, decorations, and pieces of military equipment such as helmets, arrows, and shields fashioned out of bronze. Urartian smiths were apparently also very skilled in silver and gold craft. Vases, medallions, and amulets were fashioned from silver, while gold was used to create articles of jewelry. The Urartian smiths' specialty was decorating metal with mythological and animal forms.

Left: **Carving a *khatchkar*, or memorial stone, an Armenian specialty.**

Opposite: **A statue of painter Martiros Sarian in a park in Yerevan.**

The Church of Aghthamar on Lake Van (in present-day Turkey) is the best-known extant example of the Arab and Islamic influence on Armenian architecture.

ARCHITECTURE

Churches provided the main form of architectural expression in early Armenia. The seventh century was the golden age of Armenian ecclesiastical architecture. A great many cathedrals and monuments with interior frescoes and stone carvings relating to biblical stories were constructed. The best-known is the palace church of Zvartnots, erected by Catholicos Nerses III of Ishkhan between 643 and 652. Now in ruins, the church was a circular domed structure 148 feet (45 m) high and 118 feet (36 m) in diameter. The pillars within had carvings of birds and intricate geometrical designs. The remains of the walls and the foundations can still be seen.

The Arab occupation of Armenia did not impose a halt in church building. In fact, Zvartnots was built after the Arab invasions. Another renowned church built in this period is the Church of the Holy Cross on the island of Aghthamar, at the southeastern corner of Lake Van in what is now Turkey. The chief glory of this building is its sculptures, which hold a central position in the art history of the Middle East and are important for the understanding of Christian and Islamic art of the period. Many of them bear a striking resemblance to themes found in contemporary Muslim art—for example, the biblical king of Assyria dressed as a turbaned Arab prince.

Its grandest expression is the Ani Cathedral. Built by world-famous Armenian architect Tiridates (also known as Trdat) under the sponsorship of King Gagik I, its colossal dome is 100 feet (30 m) in diameter with a crown 180 feet (55 m) above the floor.

SCULPTURE

Armenian sculptors have left their mark in stone, wood, ivory, and metal. The production of *khatchkars* (KAHCH-kahrs), or memorial stones, by Armenians is unparalleled in the art world. *Khatchkars* attained artistic excellence in the ninth to 11th centuries and are found in hundreds in graveyards and also near monasteries and cathedrals. They are rectangular, with the cross motif carved in relief in the central panel. The varieties are endless; hardly any are duplicates.

The most eminent sculptor of stone in the modern period is Ervand Kochar, creator of the equestrian statue of the legendary hero David of Sassoun.

Armenian wood-carvers have created column capitals (the top part of a column) and church doors, some of which are a thousand years old. Armenians are also known as skillful artisans in silver and gold jewelry. The few earliest examples of Armenian metalwork can be found in the museum at the rear of Echmiadzin Cathedral; in the State Historical Museum of Armenia, Republic Square, Yerevan; in the treasury of the Armenian Patriarchate of Jerusalem; and in the treasury of the Catholicossate of Cilicia, now established at Antelias, close to Beirut, Lebanon.

PAINTING

Armenian art finds its most vivid expression in the illuminated manuscripts of the Middle Ages, produced around A.D. 600. When Christian texts

HOVHANNES AIVAZOUSKY (1817–1900)

Hovhannes Aivazousky's talent as a painter won early recognition. In 1833 he was admitted to the Academy of Fine Arts in Saint Petersburg, Russia, where he won several awards. From 1840 to 1844, he finished his studies in Italy, where he painted many delightful Venetian scenes. After this he set out on a voyage around Asia Minor and the islands of the Greek archipelago. The favorite subjects of his paintings were scenes of naval battles and of storms, thunder, and lightning at sea.

In 1869 Aivazousky took part in the ceremonial opening of the Suez Canal in Egypt. From this experience he painted a general panorama of the canal and a series of pictures depicting the landscape of Egypt and the customs of the people, with a background of pyramids, sphinxes, and camels. At the age of 81 in 1898, Aivazousky completed his masterpiece, *Amid the Waves.*

The works of Martiros Saryan are exhibited in galleries around the world.

were translated into Armenian, symbolic illustrations and introductory folios were added. The manuscripts were used in religious services.

Armenia's most renowned miniature painter was Toros Roslin, who worked at Hromkla and at Sis between 1260 and 1270. Hailed as the precursor of the Italian Renaissance, Roslin has an honored place in world art history. His works are kept in the Armenian Patriarchate in Jerusalem. Another famous Armenian painter was Arshille Gorky, whose family fled to America after Turkish activities in World War I endangered them in Armenia.

The 19th century saw a dramatic change in Armenian art. The most remarkable Armenian painter of this century was Hovhannes Aivazousky. A native of Theodosia in the Crimea, Aivazousky is described as one of the world's most thrilling and prolific masters of marine pictures. He gave his favorite works to the art gallery he founded in Theodosia.

The 20th century witnessed another dramatic change in Armenian art. The trend in Armenian painting became one of portraying optimism, joyfulness, and beauty, begun by the founder of contemporary Armenian painting, Martiros Saryan (1880–1972). Saryan's paintings became associated with Armenia itself—his landscapes, characters, and subjects became symbols of the country.

RUGS AND CARPETS

Armenian rugs and carpets are world renowned. The most common are the Kazakh and Karabakh rugs. These in turn can be classified into several well-defined categories, usually named after the individual villages and districts where they are made.

Well-known Kazakh carpets originate from Lambalo, Shulaveri, the Borchalo district, and Lori-Pambakh. Modern Kazakh rugs generally have large, bold designs and clear uniformity of color. They have a high pile. Kazakh rugs are usually heavy and dense, giving the feel of substantial body.

Armenian rugs and carpets go on sale at a weekend market in Yerevan.

Karabakh rugs are similar to Kazakh ones, though the pile is often closer and the stitch finer. They show heavy Persian influence, being less stylized and geometrical than Kazakh rugs. Popular Karabakh rugs are the Lampa-Karabakh or Karadagh, which bear a resemblance to Persian rugs; Khan-Karabakh, which are mostly prayer rugs; Kazin-Ushag carpets, which have colorful plant and geometrical forms; and Channikh rugs, which often have a blue-black base color and fine stitching.

MUSIC

Armenia's long history in music can be traced in sculptures and architectural ornaments that show musicians playing various instruments and medieval manuscripts featuring figures playing pipes and flutes.

KOMITAS (1869–1935)

Komitas (Soghomon Soghomanian) was born at Kutina in Western Anatolia. He studied music and philosophy in Leipzig and Berlin before becoming a *vardapet* in the Armenian Church.

Komitas won global recognition for attracting renewed attention to Armenian national musical traditions. He collected more than 3,000 Armenian, Kurdish, Turkish, and Iranian folk songs and melodies. His original compositions, including choral works and compositions for orchestras and solo instruments, were published in a 12-volume edition.

Komitas's last public appearance in Western Europe was in 1914, in Paris, France, where he gave demonstrations of Armenian music at an international conference of musicologists. In 1915 he was arrested in Istanbul and tortured by the Ottomans. While he was spared the fate of many of his friends, upon his return to Constantinople he found his life's work—manuscripts, research findings on the *khaz* (khahz) notation system (Armenian pneumatic notation of the 11th century), and his library—in disarray. This plus his distress for the 1.5 million Armenians killed brought on a nervous breakdown. Komitas ended his days at an asylum in Paris. His remains were repatriated to Soviet Armenia and lie in state in Yerevan, where his grave is a national shrine.

Armenia has produced several outstanding composers who have made their mark on the musical scene in Istanbul, Saint Petersburg, and Tbilisi. Some renowned names are Tigran Chukhajian—who was called the Armenian Verdi for his masterpiece, the grand opera *Arshak II*—and Armen Tigranian, whose lyric drama *Anoush* is taken from the poem by Hovhannes Tumanian.

Armenia's contribution to the music scene lives on today in the likes of sopranos Lucine Zakarian, Gohar Gasparian, and Lucine Amara.

LITERATURE

Armenian literature began to develop with the creation of the Armenian alphabet in A.D. 405 and the subsequent translation of the Bible. *The History*

ENGLISH-LANGUAGE WRITERS OF ARMENIAN DESCENT

There are several well-known Armenian authors who wrote in English and other foreign languages, such as William Saroyan. One of the most distinctive was Dikran Kouyoumdjian, whose pen name was Michael Arlen. Arlen's most famous work was the novel *The Green Hat*.

The novel aroused considerable interest as a satirical chronicle of the scandalous life of the "smart set" of the 1920s and was highly shocking when it first appeared. The story concerns the green hat worn by a lively lady named Iris Storm, dressed for fun and seated in her yellow Hispano-Suiza, in which she finally commits suicide by crashing the car into a tree after her life crashes around her.

of the Armenians by Movses Khorenatsi (Moses of Khoren), attributed to the fifth century but possibly composed later, is considered one of the most important Armenian works of historiography. In addition to its considerable historical value, it is a prime source of information concerning the epics, legends, and folklore of ancient Armenia.

Through the centuries, hymns of religious inspiration were written by Armenians, including Gregory of Narek's *Book of Lamentations* and Saint Nerses Shnorhali's *Lamentations on the Fall of Edessa*.

Khatchatour Abovian was the first author to adopt a modern style. His novel, *The Wounds of Armenia*, tells of the people's suffering under foreign domination.

Among 19th-century novelists, the best known is Raffi (Akop Melik-Akopian), the Armenian romanticist. His works evoke the grandeur of Armenia's past.

Opportunities for writers were more curtailed under Soviet rule. A well-known pioneer of Soviet Armenian literature is Eghishe Charents, a poet whose works are filled with powerful symbolism. He was jailed by Stalin and died in prison in 1937. There is a museum dedicated to him in Yerevan and a village named after him in Armenia. One of his most famous poems is "Mahvan Tesil" ("A Vision of Death").

Above: **A memorial to Moses of Khoren, an Armenian historiographer.**

Opposite: **Armenian Aram Khachaturian (1903–78) composed and conducted operatic and orchestral music.**

LEISURE

ARMENIANS ARE ACTIVE people who enjoy a wide range of sports. The competitive environment of excellence in international sports is prevalent in all sports in Armenia. Armenians are also enthusiastic and avid soccer fans. Soccer games are held in stadiums, back alleys, and yards in residential areas. The country's mountainous terrain presents a haven for avid mountain climbers. Armenians have also made a name for themselves in the international chess world, having produced many grandmasters.

Above: **Playing basketball in the school gym.**

Opposite: **Spending a warm summer evening resting and sharing personal encounters among friends and neighbors.**

SPORTS

In the 1996 Atlanta Olympics, the Armenian team proudly returned home with a gold and a silver medal in wrestling. The country was represented in 11 events at the Olympics, including freestyle and Greco-Roman wrestling, swimming, track and field, cycling, weightlifting, boxing, tennis, and diving.

Armenians who have made their mark in sports at the international level were inspired by the same circumstances as other athletes of the former Soviet Union. They participated in many of the same events and trained under a united political climate. But Armenia's success at the 1996 Olympics confirms the Armenians' capability to perform independently in any field. Apart from the 60-member Olympic delegation sent by Armenia to the Atlanta Olympics, other ethnic Armenians not competing for Armenia included Andre Agassi (tennis, United States), Armen

Armenian soccer players (in red jerseys) in a World Cup European zone group one qualifier match against Finland (in white) in Tampere, Finland.

Baghdasarov (judo, Uzbekistan), Yurik Sarkisian (weightlifting, Australia), and Andrei Sarafian (100-m kayaking, Kazakhstan).

CHESS

In Armenia, as in other former Soviet republics, chess has become more than a leisure activity. For some it's a means of living.

In the 18th and early 19th centuries, the French dominated the world of chess. But it was the Soviet Union that brought it to the world's attention, especially after the 1917 revolution. The Communist government hosted many important chess events and began a program of chess education for children, providing financial support for many of its best players. As a result, players from the former Soviet republics have long dominated the game. The only hiccup was when Bobby Fischer of the United States

Armenia's chess grandmasters include Rafael Vaganian, Vladimir Akopian, Smbat Lputian, Ashot Anastasian, Artashes Minasian, Arshak Petrosian, and Genrik Kasparian.

won the world championship in 1972. Even though the Soviet Union ceased to exist in 1991, the world's finest chess players are still the ones trained under the Soviet system.

Chess is practically the national sport of Armenia, with both adults and children indulging in it. Children are educated in the finer points of chess at an early age. Many continue to pursue the game in more serious study. Chess as a form of education is highly encouraged. It is, therefore, not surprising that Armenia produces a plethora of chess champions and grandmasters.

Chess legend Gary Kasparov pits his chess genius against a virtual reality computer program in New York. Born to an Armenian mother and a Jewish father, Kasparov became world junior champion at the age of 16.

Armenia's chess grandmasters are revered by Armenians and regarded as national treasures. The accolades presented to them include the naming of streets, schools, and chess palaces after them.

A famous chess palace is named after Tigran Petrosian, who placed the first stone at its foundation himself. He was the ninth world champion. His reign lasted for seven years, from 1963 to 1969. As a further tribute to him, the Armenians erected his statue near the chess palace, and one of the main streets of Yerevan has been named after him.

To encourage young chess players in Armenia, schools, clubs, and societies have sprouted all over the country (especially in Yerevan) and have produced prodigies such as Vladimir Kopian, three-time world champion among juniors. Others include Elina Danielian, twice world champion among girls, and Levon Aronian, world champion in the junior boys' group.

Armenia hosts many regional and international chess events.

THE GAME OF CHESS

Chess traces its history to sixth-century India, where it was called *chatarunga* (chah-tah-ROONG-gah), a Sanskrit word referring to the four divisions of the Indian army. *Chatarunga* later metamorphosed into the Arabic word *shatranj* (shah-TRAHNJ). The game eventually became known as chess when it was introduced to Europe by the Moors.

Chess is played on a board of alternating light and dark squares, which are referred to as white and black regardless of the actual colors. Each side consists of an army of eight pawns and eight other pieces—a king, a queen, two rooks, two bishops, and two knights. The game requires analytical skill in strategic moves and is won by reason and deduction. It is often referred to as a game of kinsmen and is one of the few intellectually stimulating sports. A typical chess game lasts for hours.

Indulging in a friendly game of backgammon, a popular board game in Armenia. Variations allow any number of individuals to play the game, although only two people actually roll the dice and move the counters. The other players offer advice.

BACKGAMMON

A common pastime among Armenians is a slow, lazy game of backgammon, which is played at almost any time of the day or night in just about any environment—in the comfort of one's home, in the busy surroundings of a café, or under the shade of a tree.

Backgammon is probably the oldest game in recorded history. It is believed to have originated in Mesopotamia. Excavated relics and literary references indicate the game's popularity among the ancient aristocracies of Greece, Italy, Persia, and East Asia.

Backgammon requires two players, who move 15 pieces on a specially marked board according to throws of dice. The pieces, black and white or two other contrasting colors, are called stones or men. They are set out on a board divided into halves—called the inner and outer tables—by a partition. The tables are marked by 12 elongated triangles called points. The object of the game is to be the first to move all 15 stones from point to point into one's own inner table and then off the board.

109

FESTIVALS

AS ARMENIA'S POPULATION is predominantly Christian, most Armenian festivals, such as Easter and Christmas, are associated with Christianity. However, these Christian festivals are celebrated in Armenia on different days than in some other parts of the world.

In addition to the traditional Christian festivals, Armenians commemorate the Armenian genocide of 1915. Also remembered on this day are all Armenians who had been killed due to persecution or in the service of Armenia, such as those soldiers who died fighting for Armenian control over the disputed territory of Nagorno-Karabakh.

Armenians also celebrate worldwide holidays, such as New Year's Day and Mother's Day, both of which are public holidays.

Above: **Ecumenical ceremony conducted at the Armenian Genocide Monument in Tsitserna-kaberd, Yerevan.**

Opposite: **An Easter procession at Echmiadzin.**

CHRISTMAS

On January 6 the Armenian Church celebrates the Feast of Theophany (revelation or manifestation of God) as it was celebrated by the ancient churches. This is an all-encompassing celebration of the birth of Christ, the adoration of the Magi, Christ's baptism, and the revelations by the Jordan River. In the fourth century, the Syriac, Latin, and Greek churches changed the Feast of Theophany into two distinct festivals: Christ's birth (Christmas) and Christ's baptism (Epiphany). The Roman Church fixed the date of Christmas on December 25 in order to gradually replace the pre-Christian festival of the Dies Natalis Invicti Solis ("Birth of the Unconquered Sun," or winter solstice).

The selection of this date had a double significance: the celebration of Christ's birthday and the symbolic victory of Christianity over an earlier religion.

THE FEAST OF THE ASSUMPTION OF MARY

The Feast of the Assumption of Mary is celebrated by all members of the Armenian Church regardless of the country in which they reside. Celebrated in August, the Feast of the Assumption has been tied to the ritual of the Blessing of the Grapes since early Armenian Christian times.

Armenian tradition holds that about 15 years after the Resurrection, the Virgin Mary died in Jerusalem attended by all the apostles except Bartholomew (a founder of the Christian Church in Armenia). Mary was laid to rest by the apostles in a funeral conducted with great piety.

For three days and nights, the apostles remained by Mary's tomb, where they could hear angelic choirs singing. When Bartholomew at last arrived at the place where she was buried, he pleaded with the other apostles to let him see her. When he had finally convinced them to agree, they opened the tomb and found that it was empty. The adherents of the Armenian Church believe that her body had been taken to heaven.

Armenians celebrate this day in church by singing special hymns written more than a thousand years ago. Bunches of green grapes are blessed by the priest and distributed to churchgoers. Many take the blessed grapes home and share them with members of their extended family.

A choir boy all dressed up in his ecclesiastical Christmas finery, listening to Mass.

LENT

For Christians, Lent is a 40-day penitential period of prayer and fasting that precedes Easter. In the Western Church, observance of Lent begins six and a half weeks prior to Easter, on Ash Wednesday. Sundays are not counted as part of the 40 days.

In the Eastern Church, Lent extends over seven weeks because both Saturdays and Sundays are excluded. Lent used to be a period of severe fasting—only one full meal a day was allowed, and meat, fish, eggs, and milk products were forbidden. Today, however, prayer and works of charity are emphasized. Lent has been observed since the fourth century.

Novices leading the procession to pick grapes for the Blessing of the Grapes to distribute to churchgoers. Many Armenians do not buy grapes during the summertime before this day. Celebrations often continue throughout the day with picnic gatherings.

EASTER GREETINGS

In the early centuries of Christianity, the faithful embraced each other with the Latin greeting *"surrexit Dominus vere"* ("Christ is truly risen"), to which the answer was *"Deo gratias"* ("Thanks be to God"). The greeting used by Armenians for Easter is *"Kristos hareav I merelots"* ("Christ has risen from the dead"); the response is *"Orhneal e harutiwnn Kristosi"* ("Blessed is the resurrection of Christ"). In the Greek Church, the greeting is *"Kristos aneste"* ("Christ is risen"); the answer, *"Alethos aneste"* ("He is truly risen"). This greeting is still in general use by Russians, Armenians, and Ukrainians.

In Russia the Easter kiss was bestowed during matins before the night mass. People would embrace each other in church. All through Easter week, the mutual kiss and embrace were repeated not only in homes but also on the streets, even with strangers. The Poles and western Slavs greet each other with the wish *"Wesolego Alleluja"* ("A joyful alleluia to you").

In medieval times, when the bishop celebrated Easter Mass in his cathedral and the clergy received Communion from his hand, the priests and ministers would kiss him on the cheek after Communion.

EASTER

This feast celebrates the resurrection of Jesus Christ. The spring festival has its roots in the Jewish Passover, which commemorates Israel's deliverance from the bondage of Egypt. For Christians everywhere Easter marks the crucifixion of Jesus during Passover (c. A.D. 30) and the proclamation of his Resurrection three days later.

Early Christians observed Easter on the same day as the first day of Passover. In the second century, the Christian celebration was transferred to Sunday if the actual day fell on a weekday. Originally Easter commemorated both the Crucifixion and the Resurrection. It was only in the fourth century that Good Friday became a separate commemoration of the death of Christ. Easter was thereafter devoted exclusively to the Resurrection.

Easter is currently celebrated on the first Sunday after the full moon on or after March 21. The Eastern Orthodox churches follow the Julian rather than the Gregorian calendar, so their celebration usually falls several weeks after the Western Easter. In Armenia, however, Easter is celebrated on the same day as the Western Easter.

In the Armenian Church, services on Easter Sunday begin at midnight with a procession. The priest and the congregation, holding lighted candles, leave the church by a side door and walk around to the main door of the church. The main door is closed to represent the sealed tomb of Christ. When the priest makes the sign of the cross with the crucifix he holds, the doors swing open, and the congregation starts singing hymns. The church bells ring, and the procession moves into the brightly lit church. Then the Easter Mass and Communion are celebrated.

The Catholicos of All Armenians at an Easter procession.

ANCIENT CALENDARS

The earliest complete calendars were probably based on lunar observations. The moon's phases occur over an easily observed interval, the month; religious authorities declared a month to have begun when they first saw the new crescent moon.

During cloudy weather, when it was impossible to see the moon, the beginning of the month was determined by calculation. The interval from new moon to new moon, called a synodic month, is about 29.53 days. Hence calendar months contained either 29 or 30 days. Twelve lunar months (354.36 days) form a lunar year.

To keep in step with the sun, lunar-solar calendars were formed by adding an additional month when the observation of crops made it necessary. Hundreds of such calendars, with variations, were formed at various times in such diverse areas as Mesopotamia, Greece, Rome, India, and China. The month was not always based on the phases of the moon; the Mayan calendar divided the year into 18 20-day months, with a five-day period left over at the end.

THE YEAR

In ancient calendars, years were generally numbered according to the year of a ruler's reign. Around A.D. 525, a monk named Dionysius Exiguus suggested that years be counted from the birth of Christ, which was designated A.D. (Anno Domini, meaning "the year of the Lord") 1. This proposal came to be adopted throughout Christendom during the next 500 years.

THE JULIAN CALENDAR

Romans used various lunar-solar calendars. The Roman calendar was in error by several months during the reign of Julius Caesar, who recognized the need for a stable, predictable calendar and formed one with the help of an astronomer, Sosigenes. The year 46 B.C. was given 445 days, to compensate for past errors, and every common year thereafter was to have 365 days. Every fourth year, starting with 45 B.C., was to be designated a leap year of 366 days, during which February, which commonly had 28 days, was extended by one day. This was not correctly applied at first but was corrected by Augustus Caesar by A.D. 8.

THE GREGORIAN CALENDAR

The Julian leap-year rule created three leap years too many every 385 years, and equinoxes and solstices drifted away from their assigned calendar dates. As the spring equinox determines Easter, the Church was concerned, and Pope Gregory XIII, with the help of astronomer Christopher Clavius (1537–1612), introduced what is now called the Gregorian calendar. Thursday, October 4, 1582 (Julian), was followed by Friday, October 15, 1582 (Gregorian).

In the Gregorian calendar, leap years occur in years divisible by 4, except years ending in 00, which must be divisible by 400. The years 1984 and 2000 were leap years, but 1800 and 1900 were not.

ANCIENT CALENDARS (...*continued from previous page.*)

The Gregorian calendar is calculated without reference to the moon. However, the Gregorian calendar includes rules for determining the date of Easter and other religious holidays that are based on both the sun and the moon. The Gregorian calendar was adopted by Roman Catholic countries and, eventually, by every Western country and Japan, Egypt, and China.

The Armenians also had their own calendar whose reckoning begins with the year 551. For instance, year 10 on the Armenia calendar was A.D. 561 on the Gregorian calendar.

THE YEAR BEGINNING

The Roman year began in March; December, whose name is derived from the Latin word for "ten," was the 10th month. In 153 B.C., Roman consuls began taking office on January 1, which became the beginning of the year. The Julian and Gregorian calendars retained this practice.

THE ORTHODOX CHRISTIAN CALENDAR

Up to the end of World War I, all Orthodox churches used the Julian calendar. In 1923 an Inter-Orthodox Congress held in Constantinople (modern Istanbul) introduced revisions to the Julian calendar so that it corresponded to the Gregorian calendar. This New Style, or revised, Julian calendar was adopted by some Orthodox churches, while others retained the Old Style Julian calendar. The Armenian Church bases its year on the New Style calendar.

EREBOUNI YEREVAN

Of lesser importance than the Christian festivals but celebrated with just as much zest is the festival of Erebouni Yerevan, or the birthday of the capital city, Yerevan.

Erebouni Yerevan is an exciting and colorful festival. Celebrated with much gaiety, it commemorates the city's birth almost 3,000 years ago and its developments over the years. The festival is usually celebrated on the first Sunday of October.

Yerevan was founded in 782 B.C. by the Urartian king Argishti I. The ancient name of the city was Erebouni. The festival starts at Erebouni Square, where the remains of the old city are still well preserved. The events of Yerevan's long history are realistically re-created through theatrical performances and lively Armenian dances. The celebrations take place all day, and everyone in the city participates enthusiastically.

Erebouni Yerevan used to be a gala affair, but the country's economic problems in recent years have led to a cut in spending on the event.

PEACE DAY

While a Soviet republic, Armenia used to celebrate Peace Day, as did all the other Soviet republics. Peace Day, May 9, commemorated the victory of the Soviet army over the forces of Nazi Germany. It was observed with a public holiday and parades honoring the soldiers who died during World War II. Since the breakup of the Soviet Union, however, Armenia no longer celebrates Peace Day.

INDEPENDENCE DAY

Observed with a public holiday and parades, Independence Day, September 21, commemorates Armenia's independence from the former Soviet Union.

Soldiers on parade for Independence Day.

MARTYRS' DAY

Martyrs' Day marks the Armenian genocide of 1915, when 1.5 million Armenians were killed in Turkey.

Massive throngs of people usually gather at Armenia's capital, Yerevan, where they march through the city and lay flowers at an eternal flame to the victims of the genocide. The Tsitsernakaberd Park is a monument in Yerevan that was built in remembrance of the victims of the genocide. All government and church officials gather at the monument on that day.

Also remembered on this day are Armenians who died in the late 19th century at the hands of the Turks and Armenian soldiers who lost their lives in the service of their country.

A Martyrs' Day remembrance ceremony at the Genocide Memorial in Yerevan attended by then-president Levon Ter-Petrosyan and officiated by the Catholicos of All Armenians.

FOOD

ARMENIAN CUISINE IS highly refined and varied. The original nucleus of local recipes was greatly enriched over the centuries as Armenians moved from one place to another. It is impossible to say whether the dishes were originated by the Armenians and then spread to neighboring countries during their many migrations or if the cuisine was shaped by an incredible mixture of foreign influences.

Spices play an important role in Armenian cooking. Walking into an Armenian marketplace, one immediately notices the smell of a variety of spices. There is the tart, pungent fragrance of crushed barberry, the cool sweetness of dried mint, and the unmistakable fragrance of fresh basil—all of which create an unforgettable experience, especially for the cook at heart.

Left: **A popular weekend morning activity in Armenia is buying fresh fruit and vegetables at a farmers' market.**

Opposite: **An Armenian woman selling sweets outside the entrance to a monastery. Many older Armenians supplement their family's income by selling food on the street.**

A VARIED CUISINE

Armenian cuisine offers a wide variety of dishes with meat and vegetarian plates. Armenians are fond of stuffed vegetables called *tolmas* (TOLL-mahs). They stuff almost any vegetable and many fruits as well—tomatoes, eggplants, zucchinis, bell peppers, cabbage leaves, grape leaves, pumpkins, squashes, quinces, and apples. This passion for stuffed vegetables reaches its apex in a dish of assorted stuffed eggplants, bell peppers, tomatoes, and cabbage leaves called *Echmiadzin tolma.*

Because abstaining from eating meat during certain times of the year is a very important requirement of the Armenian Church, Armenians came up with many vegetarian recipes. One of the most popular is *pasus* (pah-SOOS) *tolmas* (meaning "fasting *tolmas*"), which consist of cabbage or grape leaves

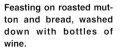

Feasting on roasted mutton and bread, washed down with bottles of wine.

stuffed with ingredients such as beans, chickpeas, lentils, rice, potatoes, and herbs.

Guests at an Armenian meal should be prepared for a feast that lasts several hours. Among the *meza* (MEH-zah), or appetizers, will likely be spicy dried meats called *basturma* (BAHS-toor-mah), *tolmas*, tasty meatballs with raisins and pine nuts, and home-cured olives.

Other popular dishes are *plaki* (PLAH-kee), a vegetable or fish stew with tomatoes, onions, and olive oil; fluffy pastries called *bourek* (boo-RAKE), filled with meat, cheese, or spinach; spicy sausages called *sudjuk* (soo-JOOK); and pieces of meat on skewers, cooked over a charcoal fire, called kebobs. Armenians often sip *raki* (RAH-kee), an anise-flavored drink, or one of the fine cognacs or wines produced in Armenia. Armenian cuisine also includes a wide selection of soups and stews. These range from richly flavored vegetarian and meat soups to simple vegetable-and-yogurt soups. Yogurt is found at every Armenian meal. In the summer it is served in the form of a cold yogurt-based soup. At other times of the year *jajik* (JAH-jeek), a very popular yogurt-and-cucumber dip, accompanies practically every dish.

Armenian meals traditionally end with servings of fresh fruit and Armenian coffee, which is brewed in a traditional long-handled brass pot similar to those used in Turkey and the Arab states.

These yogurt sellers do not have to worry about selling their product—yogurt in the form of yogurt-based soups or dips is present at every Armenian meal.

123

CHEESE

Cheese, called *panir* (pah-NEER), is a popular ingredient in Armenian cooking. Armenia produces several types of cheese, the most popular of which is a white cheese called *brindza* (BRIN-zah), made from sheep's milk. The Armenians often eat cheese on its own or wrapped in the Armenian flatbread, *lavash* (LAH-vosh), sprinkled with herbs, green onions, and tomatoes. At typical Armenian meals, it is traditional practice to have cheese served with assorted pickles called *ttu* (te-TOO) and *turshi* (TOOR-she).

An Armenian woman stacking freshly baked *lavash* that are typically enjoyed with cheese in Armenia.

HOW CHEESE IS MADE

Cheese making is an ancient craft. Even by today's standards of industrial technology, the process of cheese making, which combines art and science, remains complicated. Milk from different mammals results in variations in the types of cheese. For example, milk containing high total solids (such as milk from sheep) increases cheese yields, while milk high in fat produces softer cheese. The cheese-making process has to be modified in relation to the type of milk used.

Cheese making capitalizes on the curdling of milk. The milk is carefully selected to ensure that there are no harmful agents that could affect the process. It is heated and held at a specific temperature for a short period to destroy any harmful bacteria. Special starter cultures added to the warm milk change a small amount of the milk sugar into lactic acid. This acidifies the milk and prepares it for the next stage. Rennet (an enzyme from the stomach of a milk-fed calf) is added to the milk, and within a short time curd is produced. The curd is cut into small cubes and heated to start a shrinking process that changes it into small rice-size grains.

At a carefully chosen point the curd grains are allowed to fall to the bottom of the cheese vat. The leftover liquid consisting of water, milk sugar, and whey is drained off, and the curd grains are allowed to mat together to form large slabs of cheese. The slabs are milled, and salt is added to provide flavor and help preserve the cheese. Later it is pressed and packed into different-size containers for maturing.

COFFEE

Coffee is traditionally served in a *jezveh* (JAYS-veh), a small copper or brass coffeepot. The pot is almost figurelike in shape—wide at the top, tapering in the middle, and wide again at the bottom. A good-size spout makes pouring easy. The pot has a long handle and no lid. *Jezveh* are also available in enamelware and come in various sizes, from a single-cup size to larger ones for six cups.

A traditional Armenian coffee recipe requires water to be brought to a boil in either a *jezveh* or a saucepan. The heat is then reduced, and coffee and sugar are added. After the coffee and sugar have dissolved, the liquid is stirred for a few minutes until a thick black foam begins to rise. When this happens, the saucepan or *jezveh* is removed from the heat, and the foam is spooned into each cup before the coffee is poured.

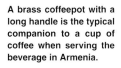

A brass coffeepot with a long handle is the typical companion to a cup of coffee when serving the beverage in Armenia.

BREAD

Lavash, or Armenian flatbread, is traditionally served during all meals. A round, thin, crisp bread, it is sometimes called Armenian cracker bread. It comes in a soft version as well and can be found in various sizes, ranging from 6 to 14 inches (15–36 cm) in diameter.

The bread is baked in a *tonir* (toe-NEER), which is a large hole dug in the ground with burning charcoal placed at the bottom. To bake the bread, the cook slaps flat pieces of dough on the already heated inner sides of the *tonir*. Once the bread is baked, it falls to the bottom of the oven and is retrieved with a pair of tongs.

Lavash is often used to make an *aram* sandwich. A softened *lavash* is spread with cream cheese, then layered with sandwich fillings such as meat, cheese, lettuce, and pickles. The *lavash* is then rolled jelly-roll style, wrapped in plastic wrap, and refrigerated for several hours. Before being served, the roll is cut into inch-thick slices.

Another popular Armenian bread is pideh, *a crusty loaf.* Pideh *can be baked in conventional ovens and are often brushed with milk or sesame seeds before baking.*

127

TOASTS

It is traditional for Armenians to propose a toast at special occasions. The toasts are proposed at the beginning of the meal when all guests and key parties are present. The host then selects a *tamada* (TAH-mah-dah), a person who will lead the party and propose all the toasts during the event.

Armenian toasts differ from those of other cultures in that the *tamada* proposes an individual toast to each person present unless it is a big event such as a wedding, in which case the toasts are proposed only to the key people such as the bride and the groom and their immediate families.

Toasts are offered as a sign of respect to the people present. A traditional toast offers praise, highlighting a person's strengths and good traits. The last toast of the occasion is always given to the host and his or her family, as an expression of gratitude. It is often said the best way to find out what others think of you is to attend an Armenian dinner and await the toast!

KHASH

Khash (kha-ah-sh) is a broth made by slowly simmering the lower leg shanks and ankles of steers. In Armenia, especially in the villages, *khash* is traditionally eaten as a celebrative meal when a child is born into a family. But if that proves to be too long a wait, any excuse can be made to throw a *khash* party. It is a meal rarely eaten alone. *Khash* parties are usually held in the morning during the winter. The meal is usually served with vodka, which supposedly acts as an antibacterial agent. *Khash* parties tend to start early, around 7 A.M., and end by 10 A.M., so that the diners can retire to a long and necessary nap after the heavy meal.

Preparing *khash* takes a long time and is usually done a day before the meal. After a thorough wash, the steers' feet and haunches are soaked in water for about six hours. They are then boiled for at least eight hours until they turn into a glutinous, cholesterol-packed soup and the flesh flakes off the bones. No seasoning is added during the cooking process.

The consumption of *khash* is complex and not for the uninitiated. It is served in a midsize or large soup bowl. The bowl contains the broth and a piece of the shank full of cartilage, fat, and sinew. A proper *khash* is served with six other components: mineral water, greens, radishes, yellow chili peppers, *lavash*, and garlic. Minced garlic and salt are added as seasoning, the *lavash* is crumbled into bits and dropped into the soup bowl, and with that final touch, the *khash* is ready for consumption. (*Pictured here, a group of Armenian men sit to an enjoyable outdoor feast.*)

HERISAH

This recipe serves four.

1 cup whole hulled wheat kernels (*zezads*)
4 cups boiling water
2 cups shredded cooked chicken or turkey (can be substituted with lamb)
2 cups chicken broth
salt and pepper to taste
4 tablespoons butter

Wash the *zezads* in cool water, then drain. Boil water in a saucepan. Add the *zezads* and stir. Set the mixture aside and let the *zezads* soak overnight.

About two hours before serving, add the shredded meat and the chicken broth to the *zezads*. Cook slowly, beating the mixture with a wooden spoon or ladle until smooth and well blended. Add salt and pepper to taste. Before serving, melt the butter, then pour over each serving of *herisah*.

SHAKARISHEE

1 egg yolk
1 cup softened butter (unsalted)
1³/₄ cups sugar
2¹/₄ cups flour
¹/₂ cup finely chopped walnuts (optional)

In a large bowl, beat together the egg yolk, butter, and sugar until smooth and almost white in color. Add flour, then blend well. If you are using the nuts, add them in. Shape the mixture into small rectangles about ³/₄ inch by ¹/₂ inch. Bake the cookies in a 250°F (121°C) oven on an ungreased cookie sheet. Cookies are done when the bottoms turn pink (after 35-45 minutes). Makes 15 to 20 cookies.

A   **B**   **C**

G E O R G I A

1

Alaverdi

Odzun

SHIRAK   **LORRI**   **TAVUSH**

Gyumri   Vanadzor   Ijevan

Spitak   Dilijan

Artik   Meghradzor

2   Aparan   Sevan

▲Aragats

Aragats
(13,418 ft / 4,090 m)   Hrazdan   **AZERBAIJAN**

ARAGATSOTN   *Lake Sevan*

Aragats   Ashtarak   **KOTAYK**   Kamo

Abovyan   Gavarr

Echmiadzin

Armavir   YEREVAN   **NAGORNO-**

ARMAVIR   Metsamor   Martuni   **KARABAKH**

Arax   **GEGHARK' UNIK'**

Artashat

Artashat   **ARARAT**

Ararat   **VAYOTS DZOR**

Yeghegnadzor

▲   *Arpa*   *Vorotan*

Ararat

3   **TURKEY**

Goris

NAKHICHEVAN   **SYUNIK**

(AZERBAIJAN)

Kapan

Kadzharan

Arax

Agarak

● Capital city
● Major town
▲ Mountain peak

Feet   Meters

16,500   5,000
9,900   3,000
6,600   2,000
3,300   1,000
1,650   500
660   200
0   0

N

4   **I R A N**

MAP OF ARMENIA

ECONOMIC ARMENIA

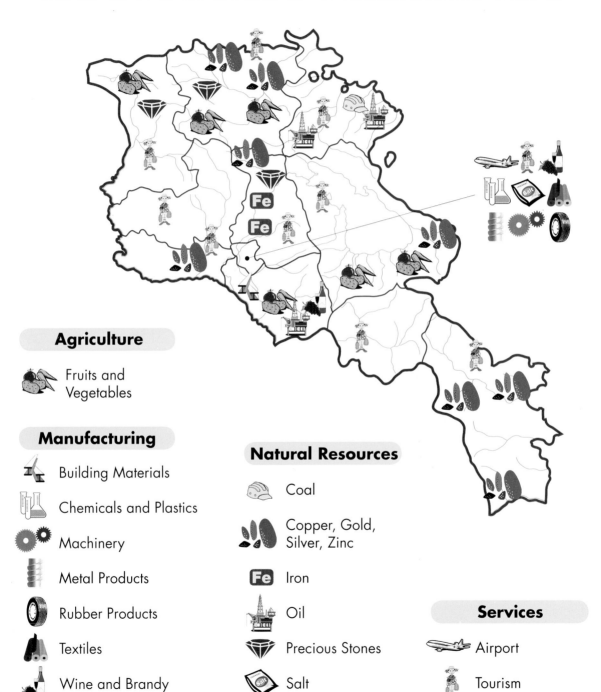

Agriculture

Fruits and Vegetables

Manufacturing

Building Materials

Chemicals and Plastics

Machinery

Metal Products

Rubber Products

Textiles

Wine and Brandy

Natural Resources

Coal

Copper, Gold, Silver, Zinc

Fe Iron

Oil

Precious Stones

Salt

Services

Airport

Tourism

ABOUT
THE ECONOMY

OVERVIEW

Due to the government's introduction of economic reforms that have helped reduce inflation and poverty, Armenia's economy has been progressing steadily during the past 10 years. This visible progress has earned Armenia support from international institutions such as the International Monetary Fund (IMF), the World Bank, and the European Bank for Reconstruction and Development (EBRD). Loans from these institutions have helped Armenia develop its economy in several sectors such as energy, agriculture, transportation, and health and education. Armenia has a diversified economy, and economic growth is supported by construction, industry, agriculture, and the service industry.

LAND AREA

11,506 square miles (29,800 square km), with 1,251 miles (2,013 km) of land boundaries. There is no coastline, as Armenia is a landlocked country.

GROSS DOMESTIC PRODUCT (GDP)

$16.94 billion (2006 estimate)

CURRENCY

dram (AMD)
Notes: 10, 25, 50, 100, 200, 500, 1,000, 5,000, and 20,000 drams
Coins (luma): 10, 20, and 50 luma
USD1 = 414.69 drams (2006)

WORKFORCE

1.2 million (2006 estimate)

UNEMPLOYMENT RATE

7.4 percent (2006 estimate)

NATURAL RESOURCES

Copper, zinc, gold, lead, aluminium, selenium; hydroelectric power; small amounts of gas and petroleum

AGRICULTURAL PRODUCTS

Fruits, vegetables, dairy, some livestock

INDUSTRIES

Chemicals, electronic products, machinery, processed food, synthetic rubber, textiles

TRADE PARTNERS

Germany, the Netherlands, Belgium, Russia, Israel, United States, Georgia, Ukraine, Iran, Romania, Turkmenistan

PIPELINES

Gas pipelines: 1,244 miles (2,002 km) (2006)

ROADS

4,743 miles (7,633 km), all of which are paved (2003)

RAILWAYS

520 miles (837 km). Some lines are out of service. About 515 miles (828 km) are electrified (2005)

HIGHWAYS

970 miles (1,561 km) (2003)

CULTURAL ARMENIA

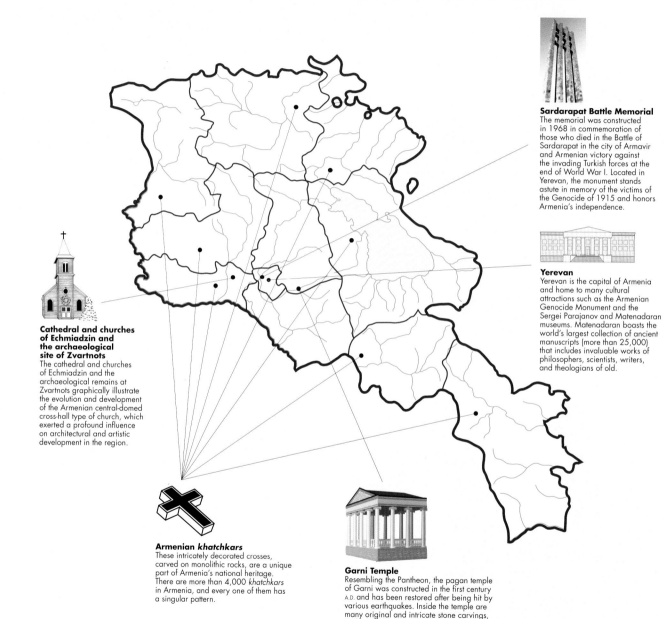

Sardarapat Battle Memorial
The memorial was constructed in 1968 in commemoration of those who died in the Battle of Sardarapat in the city of Armavir and Armenian victory against the invading Turkish forces at the end of World War I. Located in Yerevan, the monument stands astute in memory of the victims of the Genocide of 1915 and honors Armenia's independence.

Yerevan
Yerevan is the capital of Armenia and home to many cultural attractions such as the Armenian Genocide Monument and the Sergei Parajanov and Matenadaran museums. Matenadaran boasts the world's largest collection of ancient manuscripts (more than 25,000) that includes invaluable works of philosophers, scientists, writers, and theologians of old.

Cathedral and churches of Echmiadzin and the archaeological site of Zvartnots
The cathedral and churches of Echmiadzin and the archaeological remains at Zvartnots graphically illustrate the evolution and development of the Armenian central-domed cross-hall type of church, which exerted a profound influence on architectural and artistic development in the region.

Armenian *khatchkars*
These intricately decorated crosses, carved on monolithic rocks, are a unique part of Armenia's national heritage. There are more than 4,000 *khatchkars* in Armenia, and every one of them has a singular pattern.

Garni Temple
Resembling the Pantheon, the pagan temple of Garni was constructed in the first century A.D. and has been restored after being hit by various earthquakes. Inside the temple are many original and intricate stone carvings, and to its right lay the foundations and ruins of ancient residences and storehouses. The remnants of an exquisite mosaic bathhouse and the stunning view of the mountains and hills from the temple are sights to behold.

ABOUT
THE CULTURE

OFFICIAL NAME
Republic of Armenia

FLAG
Rectangular panel with three equal horizontal stripes of red, blue, and orange

COAT OF ARMS
The central shield of the coat of arms bears the charges of four royal Armenian dynasties: the Artaxids, the Arshakids, the Bagratunis, and the Rubinyans (the Kilikian Kingdom). These surround the depiction of Mount Ararat with the outline of Noah's Ark resting on the peak. The silver waves of Lake Van are at the foot of the mountain. The shield is supported by a lion and an eagle that symbolize spirit, power, forbearance, and valor. A sword at the bottom represents the struggle of the Armenian people for freedom and independence.

CAPITAL
Yerevan

OTHER CITIES
Vanadzor, Gyumri, Echmiadzin, Hrazdan, Abovyan, Armavir, Kapan, Ararat, Sevan

POPULATION
2,972,000 (2007 estimate)

BIRTHRATE
12.34 births per 1,000 Armenians (2007 estimate)

DEATH RATE
8.29 deaths per 1,000 Armenians (2007 estimate)

ETHNIC GROUPS
Armenian 97.9 percent, Yezidi (Kurd) 1.3 percent, Russian 0.5 percent, other 0.3 percent (2001 estimates)

RELIGIONS
Armenian Apostolic 94.7 percent, other Christian denominations 4.0 percent, Yezidi (monotheist with elements of nature worship) 1.3 percent

LANGUAGES
Armenian, which is spoken by the majority; Russian; English; French; German

LITERACY RATE
99.4 percent (2001 estimate)

FESTIVALS AND HOLIDAYS
Lent, Easter, Erebouni Yerevan, Independence Day, Martyrs' Day, Christmas Day

LEADERS IN POLITICS
Robert Kocharian, president of Armenia (since March 1998); Serzh Sargsyan, prime minister (since April 2007)

LEADERS IN THE ARTS
Ervand Kochar (sculptor); Toros Roslin and Hovhannes Aivazousky (painters); Soghomon Soghomanian, also known as Komitas (musician and composer); Tigran Chukhajian and Armen Tigranian (composers)

TIME LINE

IN ARMENIA	IN THE WORLD
End of first millennium B.C. Restoration of Kingdom of Armenia under King Artashes (Artaxias) II	**753** B.C. Rome is founded.
	116–17 B.C. The Roman Empire reaches its greatest extent, under Emperor Trajan (98–17).
A.D. **301** Under the reign of King Tiridates III Christianity is accepted for the Armenian people.	A.D. **600** Height of the Mayan civilization
	1000 The Chinese perfect gunpowder and begin to use it in warfare.
	1530 Beginning of transatlantic slave trade organized by the Portuguese in Africa
	1558–1603 Reign of Elizabeth I of England
	1620 Pilgrims sail the *Mayflower* to America.
	1776 U.S. Declaration of Independence
1794–96 Publication of the first Armenian periodical, *Aztarar*	**1789–99** The French Revolution
1827 Occupation of Yerevan by Russian forces	
1850 Among the schools that open in and around Yerevan, one is established exclusively for girls.	**1861** The U.S. Civil War begins.
1863 Adoption of Armenian constitution	**1869** The Suez Canal is opened.
1915 Beginning of the Armenian genocide	**1914** World War I begins.
1918 Declaration of Armenian independence	
1921 Treaty of Sevres, signed by the Ottoman government in accepting Armenia as an independent state	

IN ARMENIA	IN THE WORLD
1922 Transcaucasian Soviet Federated Socialist Republic combines Armenia, Azerbaijan, and Georgia as single republic within Soviet Union.	
1936 Armenia, Azerbaijan, and Georgia become separate republics within Soviet Union.	**1939** World War II begins.
	1945 The United States drops atomic bombs on Hiroshima and Nagasaki, Japan.
Mid-1940s–50s Several hundred thousand diasporan Armenians, many of them from the Middle East, are repatriated to Soviet Armenia under Stalin's encouragement.	**1949** The North Atlantic Treaty Organization (NATO) is formed.
1988 Beginning of movement to gain control of Nagorno-Karabakh; disastrous earthquake in northern Armenia, epicentered in Spitak, heavily damages city of Leninakan (now Gyumri).	
1991 Soviet Armenia exercises the right guaranteed in the Soviet constitution to conduct a referendum to secede from the Soviet Union and declare independence.	**1991** Breakup of the Soviet Union
1992 Armenia is admitted to the United Nations.	**1997** Hong Kong is returned to China.
2001 Celebration of 1,700th anniversary of Armenia's adoption of Christianity	**2001** Terrorists crash planes in New York, Washington, D.C., and Pennsylvania.
	2003 War in Iraq begins.

GLOSSARY

Catholicos of All Armenians
The spiritual leader of the Armenian Church

Cilicia
Kingdom founded in 1080; also known as Lesser Armenia. This is also the region of the plateau surrounding the central Taurus Mountains and the plain between the Taurus and Armanus mountains.

Greater Armenia
Kingdom founded by Artaxias in 189 B.C., which consisted of the region of northern Armenia

humus
Nutrients in the soil deposited by decaying vegetable and animal matter. Soil rich in humus is very fertile.

jezveh (JAYS-veh)
A small copper or brass vessel traditionally used to brew coffee. A *jezveh* is wide at the top, tapers in the middle, and flares out at the base. It has a spout, a long handle, and no lid.

khatchkar (KAHCH-kahr)
Rectangular memorial stone with a cross motif carved in relief as the central panel

lavash (LAH-vosh)
Armenian flatbread, usually thin and crispy and ranging from 6 to 14 inches (15–36 cm) in diameter. *Lavash* also comes in a soft version.

marl
Fertile soil with mix of calcium and clay usually formed in marine environments

meza (MEH-zah)
Appetizers served at a feast. Popular *meza* include dried meats, stuffed vegetables and fruit, and meatballs.

Parsi
An adherent of Zoroastrianism who fled persecution in Iran and settled in India

Russification
The abandonment of native customs and cultural institutions and the assimilation of Russian culture and way of life

satrapies
Provinces within the Persian Empire governed by satraps (viceroys)

tanzimat (TAHN-zee-MAHT)
Turkish word meaning "reorganization." The Tanzimat was the program of modernization and Westernization of administration undertaken by the Ottoman Empire in the late 19th century.

tolma (TOLL-mah)
Vegetable or fruit stuffed with assorted mixtures such as beans, rice, and potatoes

tonir (toe-NEER)
A large hole in the ground with burning charcoal at the bottom used as an oven to bake *lavash*

vardapets (VAHR-dah-pets)
Monastic priests in the Armenian Church

FURTHER INFORMATION

BOOKS

Balakian, Peter. *The Burning Tigris: The Armenia Genocide and America's Response.* New York: Harper Collins, 2003.

Hovannisian, R. (editor). *The Armenian People—From Ancient to Modern Times.* New York: St. Martin Press, 1997.

Manoukian, Mariam. *On the Other Side of Mount Ararat: A Story of a Vanished City.* Yerevan: Abril Publishing, 2005.

Parmelee, Ruth A. *Pioneer in the Euphrates Valley.* Princeton, NJ: Gomidas, 2000.

WEB SITES

Adventures in Armenian Cooking. www.armeniapedia.org/index.php?title=Adventures_in_Armenian_ Cooking

ArmeniaDiaspora.com. www.armeniadiaspora.com/index.asp

Armenia Statistical Data. www.armstat.am/StatData/

Armenia Tree Project. www.armeniatree.org

FlashPoints World Conflicts: Nagorno-Karabakh. www.flashpoints.info/countries-conflicts/Nagorno-Karabakh-web/Nagorno-Karabakh_briefing.html

Government of the Republic of Armenia. www.gov.am/enversion/index.html

Republic of Armenia and the IMF. www.imf.org/external/country/ARM/index.htm

Reuters AlertNet—Armenia. www.alertnet.org/db/cp/armenia.htm

World Health Organization—Armenia. www.who.int/countries/arm/en/

FILM

Ararat. Directed by Atom Egoyan. Produced by Atom Egoyan and Robert Lantos. 2002.

MUSIC

Armenian Melodies. Khatchatur Avedissian. Parseghian Records, 1999.

BIBLIOGRAPHY

Hoogasian-Villa, Susie. *One Hundred Armenian Tales*. Detroit, MI: Wayne State University Press, 1982.

Investment Climate Surveys. *Armenia*. World Bank, 2005.

Kherdin, David, and Nonny Hogragian. *The Golden Bracelet*. Boston, MA: Little Brown and Co., 1996.

Marsden, Philip. *The Crossing Place: A Journey Among the Armenians*. New York: Kodansha, 1995.

Uvezian, Sonia. *The Cuisine of Armenia*. New York: Harper & Row, 2003.

CIA World Factbook—Armenia. www.cia.gov/library/publications/the-world-factbook/geos/am.html

INDEX